A Song to Sing

Healing through Separation and Divorce

Annette Peters

Copyright © 2013 by Annette Peters

A Song to Sing
Healing through Separation and Divorce
by Annette Peters

Printed in the United States of America

ISBN 9781626972070

All rights reserved solely by the author. The author guarantees all contents are original and do not infringe upon the legal rights of any other person or work. No part of this book may be reproduced in any form without the permission of the author. The views expressed in this book are not necessarily those of the publisher.

Unless otherwise indicated, Bible quotations are taken from The New Living Translation. Copyright © 1996 by Tyndale House Publishers, Inc.

Most names have been changed.

www.xulonpress.com

This project is dedicated to anyone hurting due to separation and divorce. May my story encourage you that there truly is healing, hope and life after divorce.

Prologue

It was the moment in time that would forever change my world as I knew it. . .

Thursday, January 27, 2005

It was about 12:20 p.m. and I was busily typing a proposal at work when the phone rang. I answered with my usual cheery greeting, which was followed by my husband, Brady's voice. He said he wasn't feeling well, so he left work early today. Could I come home for lunch? Now I'll admit that my initial thoughts weren't ones of a supportive wife. Instead I selfishly thought about how it was below freezing outside and that I'd even prepared not to needlessly go out into the cold by bringing a microwavable meal for lunch. However, this was my husband asking, so instead I answered, "Sure, do you need something to eat or any medicine?" He replied that neither was needed, so I said, "I'm on my way." I saved the project on my computer and headed out into the frigid air to my vehicle for the 20-minute commute.

As I drove toward my home, my stomach started feeling funny, nauseous even, but I had no idea why (I hadn't even eaten my frozen lunch yet). Then I remembered that my oldest teen-aged daughter was home sick from school, so I imagined that she and my husband had clashed and it was time for me to put on my "mom vs. wife referee uniform." My stomach churned in anticipation. At about 1:15 p.m., I pulled into the driveway and walked anxiously to the door of our warm home. My husband greeted me at the front door. After casually taking a sip of the soft drink he held in his hand, he simply said three words that will be forever etched in my mind: "Baby, I'm leaving." *What?!* I actually braced the wall for support and I remember feeling as though I was going to collapse in a heap right there in the middle of the family room floor. (I can't help but wonder if the strong arms of God literally kept me standing upright.) It was like time stopped. . . like my heart stopped. . .

I was frozen in disbelief. . . as though I was standing in the middle of the aftermath of an implosion with the pieces of debris (my life, my dreams) falling down all around me. As soon as I could gain *some* composure, I ran to him, hugged him and desperately pleaded with him to stay, with tears streaming down my face. I begged him to tell me what was going on, to sit down and talk to me. I unashamedly continued begging him to stay. He barely spoke and unemotionally continued moving his remaining items out the door and into his truck. He let me kiss him and hug him and I remember sobbing on his shoulder. I told him how I felt that God had brought us together almost nine years ago, so He could work this out if we'd put it in His hands. I was willing to get some counseling or whatever it took, but I believed with all my heart that God had a plan for us to stay together. Brady led me to believe he only wanted a separation and he was willing to get help for the marriage.

It was soon time for me to leave to pick up my youngest daughter from school, so I gave him one last hug and kiss, put my sunglasses on to hide my tear-filled, and now mascara-less eyes, and drove away. It would be the last time I'd see Brady standing in the doorway of our home.

State of the Marriage

This was the second marriage for both of us. I have two daughters from my first marriage, and Brady has no children. I knew our marriage wasn't perfect, but I had no idea it was so bad he would pack up and leave. In the fall, some friends won a marriage weekend getaway but could not attend and offered it to us. I asked him to attend it with me, but he said "things were fine" and he did not want to go, so I didn't push it. I just figured every marriage has some stress in it, especially when it is a second marriage and there are children involved. As I look back over the last several years, we had grown apart, both doing our own thing. He didn't even attend church with me the last couple of years, claiming he was helping a friend with music at a new church he was starting. He didn't even come to the hospital when I had my gallbladder removed because he didn't want to take time off work. As usual, I acquiesced and didn't push him, afraid I'd make him angry. I just assumed in a couple of years when my daughters went off to college, things would be better between us.

There is a song about this by Casting Crowns entitled "Slow Fade."[1] Some of the lyrics are, "People never crumble in a day, families never crumble in a day, daddies never crumble in a day." Looking back, I think this sentiment applied to us.

Divorce. I hate the word itself.

Webster defines divorce as, "the action of legally dissolving a marriage". I've been told that in Greek it literally means "hard heart." Unfortunately, when I describe my life experiences, I have to include this word . . . twice! My first marriage ended in divorce 20 years ago. There is a sense of shame and failure whenever I have to admit this part of my life, wondering what people will think of me. I know "*there is no condemnation for those who are in Christ*," according to Romans 8:1, but shame is still an emotion I have to really work to reject, as I know Satan can and will use this against me whenever he can. He wants me to believe I am a loser, that something must be wrong with me if two husbands left. He wants me to believe the lie most women in our society believe . . . that I was not good enough to be loved. He wants me to camp right there, and he wants you there right along with me. I hope you'll see through this book how by God's grace, I pulled up the stakes and moved on to a better place.

This book is my story. The only reason I have even written it all down is because I know there are many other people who have been through this terrible event in their lives. My hope is that through my story, you can see God has restored me and given me hope for my future. He wants to do the same for you! There can be life, even an abundant life after divorce. Even though this period has been the most painful one in my life, it is also the time I have drawn the closest to God and learned about myself and who I really am. I want you to see that just like me, you are one of God's children and He longs for a relationship with you. He is waiting to give you a peace that surpasses understanding . . . which is exactly what He has done for me.

This book is a combination of my thoughts and lessons learned, along with actual excerpts from my journal and from other books I have read that I highly recommend (which are footnoted). My prayer is those who will be encouraged by this book will read it and discover true healing along with a love for God and the promise for an abundant life. God really does make beauty from ashes, and believe me, sometimes we have to go through the fire . . . the refiner's fire.

I

Refiner's Fire

Malachi 3:3 *"He will sit as a refiner and purifier of silver; he will purify the Levites and refine them like gold and silver."*

Let me explain what I have learned about the meaning of this verse. When a refiner, or silversmith, holds a piece of silver over the fire, he has to hold the silver in the middle of the fire where the flames are the hottest to burn away all the impurities. He has to sit there not only holding the silver, but he has to keep his eyes on the silver the entire time it is in the fire. If the silver is left a moment too long in the flames, it will be destroyed. And here is the coolest part . . . the silversmith knows the silver is fully refined when he sees his image in it!

So it occurred to me that when we are going through the toughest times (the fire), God is not only refining us (getting rid of the anger, bitterness, hurt, etc.), He is watching over us through the entire trial so closely we won't be destroyed.

He is purifying us so He can see His reflection in us. Even though we don't like it, probably how we handle the toughest events in our life actually draw us closer to God.

Divorce – the Silent Sin?

Have you ever noticed the word divorce is hardly ever spoken at church? We don't openly pray for someone going through this devastating life event as we do when someone's spouse has died. When have you ever heard an elder or minister get in the pulpit and pray for Sister Susie who is going through a divorce? But they would respectfully pray for her if her husband had just died. I don't believe they intend to be insensitive. The topic of divorce is still uncomfortable in church. The church does not like divorce obviously, so there is a fine line between supporting a person going through one without actually condoning divorce itself.

In my experience divorce is a death . . . the death of a relationship, the death of a dream, and the death of a family unit. In some ways, I believe it is harder than dealing with the death of a spouse. A grieving spouse has assurance their spouse died loving them – there was no personal rejection as with a divorce. Probably the last words were kind and loving and not ones of rejection, like a sword to the heart. This spouse has happy memories to hold on to, and even pictures to display. Divorce procedures and legal battles overshadow any happy memories that may have been made, and any photographs are destroyed or at least removed from sight. Often the surviving spouse of a death receives support from church, family and friends, including meals, visitation, flowers, phone calls, and cards. With a divorce, only the closest friends usually know what is going on, due to the shame of failure and possible fear of rejection by their church, family and friends.

A surviving spouse grieves over the loss of a spouse, best friend, lover, and life-mate. Divorce includes these same painful emotions, but, especially when there are children involved, this spouse has to continually see the one who left and rejected them, causing these painful emotions to rise up again. I believe when Jesus talked about how we need to forgive seventy times seven, it may be for times such as this when we re-live past hurts, and we have to forgive the same sin against us over and over. But you know, God does this for us daily.

We have so many brothers and sisters hurting to the core of their being because of separation and divorce! They keep it all in and try to be strong, but on the inside their hearts are breaking. I know – I've been there. I've come to church in "my Sunday best," with my hair fixed and makeup on and with such good intentions to be strong and put on a happy face, and say "I'm fine" when asked. But then a certain worship song would be sung or memory would come to me, and my tears would just flow down my face. This happened **every** Sunday morning for six months! We as a church need to come alongside these precious people and help restore them through their trauma . . . instead of judging them.

If you happen to be in a church leadership position and are separated or going through a divorce, my advice is to temporarily step down. A wise, godly man spoke those words to me after his own personal experience. I took this advice and met with one of the ministers at my church and told him of my decision to step down. Now practically, I didn't have the emotions or stamina to continue to lead a small group of middle school girls, or sing on the worship team. At my church, which has been so amazing with me, the ministers were supportive and even told me they would NOT have asked me to step down, but agreed it was a wise choice for me. You see, this was time I needed to work on healing, and, honestly, **I needed to be ministered to**. My main reason, though, was to send a message to my estranged husband that my first priority was to work on getting our marriage on track. It did not work, as you'll read, but at least I know I truly gave it my best shot.

The Day After

Friday, January 28, 2005

Mr. & Mrs. B came to our office for an appointment with my boss first thing in the morning. I tried to remain calm and professional, but when I escorted them into the conference room, Mr. B said the strangest thing. He asked me, "How is Brady? Is he happy?" (Now what kind of question is that?) I immediately started to sob and told them I guessed he was unhappy as he had left me the day before. Stunned, they sat me down and explained how they were separated for a year a few years ago but they worked things out and have a great marriage now. This gave me some hope.

Here is what I want you to see. God is in control even when we cannot see it. I believe He had already orchestrated this appointment with a couple who had previously walked in my shoes. This couple hasn't had a meeting with my boss for five years (and it wasn't even listed in our appointment book). They were the couple my husband had most connected with during a recent business trip . . . and they just happened to come to my office the day after my husband leaves! Coincidence? I don't think so.

Later I'll tell you how else God was working behind the scenes for me, but I don't want to get ahead of the story.

I returned to my desk to get back to work, and there was an email from my husband asking me if I would go with him to his parents' home for a visit on Sunday. My initial response was, "Hello . . . do you not remember you just left me yesterday!?" Mr. B was still in the office, so when I saw him before he left, he explained this is his way of testing me. . . to see if the door was open. His advice was to immediately respond to him and then go. So I did.

Sunday, January 30, 2005

Today I went with Brady to see his parents. It was apparent he hadn't told them of his decision to separate. Despite the cloud hanging over us, it was a nice visit. His mom liked her birthday gift and Brady told her the idea was his but the color and selection was mine. His dad actually said, "You all make a good team . . . always have." OK, that was weird, but I definitely remember it. Brady dropped me off at our home and drove away . . . that was weird, too. I insisted he tell his parents the next day of his decision to separate.

Sunday, February 13, 2005 (The last time we'd meet, but I don't know this at this writing)

I don't believe Brady has met someone else, and I believe he wants to try to work things out. I've started going to a counselor and Brady is supposed to schedule an appointment with one as well. I think he may be going through a mid-life crisis. Maybe he is grieving that he never had his own children and still has hurts and issues from his first marriage he never worked through and resolved.

This might be a good time for a warning for anyone who has been divorced for a while and is thinking about dating. Even if you have worked through your pain and are healing, be careful who you date. If you date someone who is also divorced, be sure they have dealt with their own pain and all that goes with divorce. If they haven't, most likely you will be a distraction from them working through their issues. You are like novacane for them, according to DivorceCare[2] professionals, so they don't have to feel the pain. But just as when novacane wears off, *they will have to deal with the pain, and so will you.*

In my case, I was single for five years between marriages. However, I was so busy working two jobs and raising my daughters I really didn't have time, energy, or even know the importance of dealing with **my** part of my first failed marriage. So I made the same mistakes in the second one.

Sunday, February 27, 2005

It's been one month since Brady left. Today I am having a bad day. It is 10:22 a.m., and I tried to call him on Friday night and then again two times this morning – no answer. So I guess we are not meeting for church and lunch today as we have done the last couple of weeks, since I haven't heard from him. I hope he is OK – it's pretty weird he is not answering his cell phone.

I think today I'm afraid he does not miss me and does not want to work things out. How will I deal with this? I feel like such a loser. But I really don't know what else I could have done – I'm exhausted. Some days lately I feel the weight of the world on top of me, knowing I am solely responsible for my daughters and their well-being and keeping our household running. What if he wants a divorce? What will I do financially? I guess it's too soon to worry about that. I know in my heart God will get me through whatever comes my way. I'm not at church today because if the people who know about this separation ask how I'm doing, I'll just burst into tears. Instead, I'm trying to get all these feelings down on paper, hoping to relieve some of the shame and grief I feel. My counselor (as well as my mom) suggested I keep a journal and include something good and bad that happened each day, as well as a problem and how I could solve it. The counselor also suggested Brady and I need to get our relationship on even ground. She said we should decide how often we'll see each other and how often and when we'll call each other; to schedule it. Right now it feels as though he has all the control and I wait to see IF he'll call me. I asked him the last time we talked on the phone if it would be OK if I called him and he said, "yes." I believe he was out of town this past Tuesday through Thursday, so I waited until Friday to call, but no answer. This makes me wonder if he has already met someone else.

I don't miss the stress of him here, but I miss what I believe our marriage could be. I miss the companionship we had at the beginning of the marriage. I'm also a little scared about being alone in the next few years if he doesn't want to work things out, as the girls will soon leave for college. I don't want to dissuade them from going if that is God's plan for them, just so I won't be alone. I don't want to hold them back – I want them to live their lives.

Is Brady trying to hurt me by not calling me? Should I ask him that? I'm afraid I'll say one wrong thing and he'll say, "That's it, I don't want to work things out." I'm still tiptoeing around his feelings. Does he hurt and feel lonely after our calls like I do? Each time he says he loves me. Has he changed his mind since the last time I saw him? Does he ever cry like I do? Does he ever cry over me?

I feel like such a loser. I've tried so hard to be such a loving, attentive, and giving wife, but obviously that hasn't been enough. Lord, please help me through this.

Monday, March 7, 2005 10:00 p.m.

Today I spoke with a new counselor named Debbie. This is another blessing from God, as one of my bosses is paying for this. Wow! She suggested I either email Brady or call him since it has been two weeks since I have heard from him. She said it was OK to let him know I am concerned about him and that I miss him. So I did just that.

Phone counselor Debbie said I'm in a "faith" part of my life. I just need to have faith God wants things to work out between us if we both work on our own character issues and this marriage could be greater than we can even imagine. So I'm trying to stay focused on being positive. She said he is testing me now, but I also feel as though I'm left hanging – like I've been shunned.

Wednesday, March 9, 2005

Tonight the girls are at a basketball game at school and I'm home . . . alone. My counselor said last night I'm not mad yet because I am grieving. I am grieving my idea of what a marriage should be, of what a husband should be, of who I thought he was. I don't understand why he keeps hurting me. I never meant to hurt him! I can't believe this marriage may not work out! Brady is a Christian man, and that was my initial attraction to him. He seemed to have a deeper relationship with Christ than I had, and I longed for that in a spouse. This separation is not from God. If we needed to separate to work things out, we should have mutually agreed to it. It's not right he just decided and planned to leave! He continues to control me. I've got to learn to stand up for myself. Just because I don't agree with everything he says doesn't mean I'm wrong.

Lord, I need your peace tonight. You know how I am . . . I like to know and plan my schedule in advance, so this not knowing what is in store for me is really hard and uncomfortable for me. This must be where my faith comes in – knowing without a doubt that You will get me through, even though I don't know all (or any) of the answers. I know Psalm 119:105 says that your word is a lamp unto my feet, giving me just enough light to illuminate a little bit of ground before me like a flashlight on a dark path. Help me to rest in that. Thank you for Your love. Amen.

II

Good Grief

The reason I entitled this section "Good Grief" is because grieving is an honorable thing to do. When someone dies, we grieve because we loved them, and will miss them and there will be a void in our life that only they could fill. We only grieve someone who meant something to us. To grieve the loss of the marriage shows we honored it; it was important to us, according to DivorceCare[2] professionals.

As uncomfortable as grieving is, it is a necessary part of healing from divorce or any other traumatic event. I wish I could tell you a textbook amount of time for this process, but it, like so many other emotions of divorce, depends on the person, the length of the marriage, and the situation.

Grief includes many emotions including, shock, denial, sadness, depression, lack of energy, and confusion. It is OK to feel these emotions. If you need to cry, by all means, do it . . . (even if you're in church). I've cried while walking on a treadmill, while driving my car (a lot), and even in the grocery store. (If you do that, just go over by the onion section).

I found the best way for me to deal with my grief was to journal (and cry). There is just something so freeing about getting all those thoughts cluttering up my head onto paper. It also allowed me to sleep at night. Journaling doesn't mean you have to go buy a pretty book and write in complete sentences. It is for your eyes only, so do it however it works for you. I'll admit sometimes I was so mad at my spouse, I wrote my thoughts in shorthand so that if I died in the middle of the night and my kids found my journal, they wouldn't be able to read it! Don't worry; I haven't included any of those entries in this book.

I also dealt with my grief by talking to my girlfriends. I can't emphasize enough the importance of having some same-sex friends in your life to help you through this life crisis. I would also encourage you to join a support group. You are not meant to go it alone! It is so healing to be in a group of people dealing with the same issues as you are, who don't judge you, can empathize with you and can even advise you from their own experiences. Much healing goes on in group settings such as these. There is a great organization nationwide called DivorceCare[2], www.divorcecare.org. On this site, you can type in your zip code and find groups that meet near you. I can't recommend this program enough! (More on that later.)

Another thing that helped me through the grieving process was to list my losses, as I learned from DivorceCare. For me, these losses included the loss of my husband (obviously), the loss of his family, our home, the immediate family, and my dreams for our future/retirement together.

Even though this grieving period is probably the hardest time in your life, I want you to know it is not a waste of time. It is usually when we are in our deepest pain that we draw the closest to God and allow Him to heal our hearts. Below are some suggestions to help you in your grieving process:

1) List your losses you need to grieve.
2) Our God is a healing God. List some examples from the Bible where He healed.
3) List your friends who would be willing to help you through this difficult time.

Sunday, March 13, 2005

Today has been a tough day. At church the sermon was about forgiveness and how much it hurts when we are betrayed by someone we love. I cried. Again. Our minister, Rick, went on to say how reconciliation and forgiveness can happen and we are commanded to forgive if we want to be forgiven. Someone said we are most like God when we forgive.

Lord, I pray I will be able to forgive Brady no matter what the outcome of this marriage is. Since I haven't heard from him in three weeks, my hope for reconciliation is slowly dying. I'm afraid he's pulling away and will get used to living without me and enjoy it. I still can't believe this has happened! Lord, I don't want a divorce and he hasn't suggested this; I'm just not certain what the silence from him is all about. Lord, you know me inside and out and you know that I feel like a loser. Help me to be a testimony for You through this time in the valley. It is often easy for us to believe during the mountaintop experiences, but how we live during the low times says volumes about who we are and the faith that we have. Help me to be bold for You. I love you. Amen.

Monday, March 28, 2005

Easter was hard. It was the two-month anniversary of when Brady left. I still have not heard from him. I sent him a note asking him to tell me what the silence means. Again, I don't miss the stress and feeling he was mad at me almost every day, but I miss having someone think I'm special and want to hold me. I want him to be gentle and caring and understanding and forgiving, but maybe he can't be those things now. I'm in the grieving process still. I feel like a failure, even though I know I must shake it. Today I was reminded love drives out fear and God loves me. I want to claim this promise and just like Leah in the Bible, maybe God is to be my love.

Wednesday, March 30, 2005

Today, when I returned home from a great-aunt's funeral, I received a letter from Brady asking for a couple of items he left in the house when he quickly packed up and left on that cold January day. He wants a couple of ceramic cereal bowls and a carrot peeler. Really?! Now I'm mad! The grief has gone, and now I am fuming mad! After almost nine years of marriage all he wants is a stupid carrot peeler and a couple of cereal bowls? How pathetic! Now I want to punch him! Am I not much more precious than these common household items, but he chooses them? Ouch.

Lord, please forgive me for my part in this mess and for my mean thoughts toward him right now. Help me to totally trust in You. For I know that You know the plans you have for me – plans to help me and not to hurt me, according to Jeremiah 29:11. Thank you for my girls and family and friends, church, and job. Lord, I pray that during this upcoming mission trip that I am to take, I will be able to focus on You and what You want us to do. Please keep us safe. Lord, again I pray for your hedge of protection around our home, as I don't know how to protect my girls, so I'll leave that to you. Love and Amen.

Anger is not a sin.

This may be a good time to address the issue of anger. I have heard people say anger is a sin but I just can't find that in my Bible. I'm pretty sure it says "not to sin in your anger," meaning that at times we are going to feel it. Jesus got angry, so I'm in good company! Remember when He went into the temple and turned over the money tables? He was incensed the temple (His Father's house of worship) was being used as a market instead of a place of prayer and worship. The difference between Jesus' anger and ours is that we have a tendency to sin. We are made to get angry at injustice such as abuse or children starving, etc., but we just have to be careful and not let that lead us to do something stupid and sin. (For example, me wanting to punch my husband's lights out because he wants a stupid carol peeler and cereal bowls!)

Looking back on my childhood, I don't ever remember seeing my mom get angry, though trust me, she had some good reasons to at times. Knowing my sweet grandma, my mom probably never saw her get angry either. I don't blame them, of course, but I think I grew up thinking anger was not an option for a woman, so I never really got angry. I must have just buried that emotion, so it was a hard emotion for me to deal with during my divorce.

Now don't get me wrong – if someone hurts one of my children, I have no problem feeling this God-given motherly emotion. As Beth Moore, an incredible speaker and Bible Study teacher would say, "I want to snatch someone bald-headed." But for some reason, if someone hurts me, it takes a while for me to feel angry. I probably need to talk to my counselor about this. . .

I am learning anger needs to be dealt with and not stuffed, because if we don't deal with it now, it will come out later. Holding on to anger just eats us up. It is not hurting the person you are angry with, but it can control you and your life. Before you know it, several years have gone by and you are still stuck in anger and bitterness. This, in turn, can hurt your other relationships. People get tired of someone stuck in their pity party after several years of not doing anything to get help. If you find yourself in this situation, get some help now. Life is too short to waste years stuck in a pit of self-pity.

The day I finally got *really* angry was the day I found out about my husband's secret life. My heart literally ached. I felt a sick combination of pain, rejection, disbelief and anger! My first reaction was to seek revenge. I planned a scheme to embarrass him in front of his co-workers. I was so excited! But when I told one of my brothers about it – I'll call him my sensible brother – he said, "That is not you. That is not something you would do. And it could be dangerous and not go according to your plan. And even if it does, you will never be able to forget the hurt look on his face. You will not be able to look yourself in the mirror again. You will live with regret." Dang. Why did I tell him and let him rain on my parade? I should have told my other brother . . . the one who would beat somebody up for me!

But in hindsight, I am so glad I told him and he was honest with me and gave me wise advice. My whole goal in life is to truly live in accordance with God's word. Even though I would have been repentant and God would have forgiven me, there would have been painful consequences. James 1:19 - 20 says, " . . . *Everyone should be quick to listen, slow to speak and slow to become angry, for man's anger does not bring about the righteous life that God desires.*"

I believe "slow to become angry" can mean to not jump to conclusions or rely on possible gossip, but to instead get all of the facts from reliable sources and then get wise advice before reacting in haste.

So how did I deal with my anger? I went to the gym and walked/ran on a treadmill, did some cardio classes and journaled a great deal. I talked to my friends (and counselor) because I needed to get it all out. I believe anger is like a poison. It is toxic to our health, our relationships and even our faith.

There are several verses in the Bible regarding how to deal with anger, and they are tough! Leviticus 19:18 says, "*Do not seek revenge or bear a grudge against one of your people, but love your neighbor as yourself.*" In the book of Nahum (Who? . . . Where did this book come from?) 1:2-3 says, "*The Lord is a jealous and avenging God; the Lord takes vengeance and is filled with wrath . . . The Lord is slow to anger and is great in power; the Lord will not leave the guilty unpunished. . .*" Now before we start pumping our fists in the air saying, "Yes, our ex is gonna get it!" we probably need to look at ourselves and see that we, too, are guilty. Even if you are what the DivorceCare[2] professionals refer to as the "innocent party" in the divorce (meaning that you did not want the divorce, or was not unfaithful in the marriage, for example) you are still guilty of sin. No one is perfect, so I take comfort knowing God is slow to get angry with me.

Probably the verse most often referred to regarding anger is Romans 12:19 – 21. "*Do not take revenge, my friends, but leave room for God's wrath, for it is written: 'It is mine to avenge; I will repay,' says the Lord.*" But I think we often stop there and become a little smug and don't continue on with the next verse, which says, "*On the contrary: If your enemy is hungry, feed him; if he is thirsty, give him something to drink. In doing this you will heap burning coals on his head. Do not be overcome by evil, but overcome evil with good.*"

Before you get too excited about the "heaping burning coals on his head" part and think that is a suggestion you could agree with, let's focus on the rest of the passage. Basically it is telling us to treat others as Christ would if He was in your shoes . . . and you know what, He has been. He was not married and didn't go through a legal separation and divorce, as we have, but He has gone through the pain of rejection and loneliness, even more than we have! Even though divorce is a time of great pain for you because you feel abandoned by a loved one, God has never left you! Yet, when Christ died on the cross, He bore our sins. Since a Holy God can't have anything to do with sin, God actually had to look away from Jesus at that time. Jesus was truly alone on that cross! So He knows how you feel. When I think about that, it is easier to pray for my ex husband . . . for good things for him, no longer that he'll move to Africa and get eaten by a lion. (Where did that come from?!)

Another part of this verse is knowing God will repay, because He is a just God, and He knows best, and He doesn't need any of my scheming to help Him out.

I heard someone speak on the topic of anger, and what he said really hit home with me. Years ago, his wife had left him and he was proud of the fact they did not fight; the legal matters went along smoothly and it was over pretty quickly. He said later that he realized that he also did not fight FOR her or for the marriage. So now his prayer is he will get angry about the things that make God angry and not about little silly things in life that have a tendency to get under our skin. Sounds like a great idea.

Questions to ponder:

1) Are you angry and why?
2) How have you dealt with this anger?
3) Do you need to change your way of dealing with anger?
4) What are some things that make God angry that should make you angry?

Sunday April 10, 2005

On my 40th birthday, a little over a week ago, I was one of several adults chaperoning a mission trip with our youth group to Mexico. We all met at church that night, and before loading the bus for our 24-hour bus ride, we had a send-off prayer in the Fellowship Hall. I remember the spouses of the other chaperones standing behind their spouse who was about to leave, with their hands on their shoulders praying for them and their protection. I felt so alone in that room. How I longed to have someone stand behind me and pray for me like that! I managed to hold back the tears, but later as we drove through the night, they escaped as I curled up in the back seat of the bus before I finally went to sleep.

I offered to go on this trip to "help with the youth," but what I didn't expect was God really wanted me there. The theme was Sojourn – the journey for truth. Does that fit where I am or what?! One of the most amazing things we did was visit ruins of a monastery built in the1700's. We worshipped there and then we lay on our backs and looked up at the gorgeous sky and amazing stars. They were so bright and beautiful, and there were thousands of them! The walls were built so tall that all we could see were the stars. All the city lights were blocked out by the height of the walls. It was an incredible sight I will never forget. I hope I won't wait so long to just be quiet in God's presence and be in awe of Him. How often we miss that. I wonder if that makes Him sad.

As I lay there, I thought how amazing that the Creator of those stars is my creator too, and He knows me personally and is concerned for me and knows my hurts and pains. I had tears streaming down my cheeks at this realization. I thought of how I need to really work on "being still and knowing that He is God." If I don't do this, how will I know His plan for the rest of my life?

Seeing all of those amazing twinkling stars reminded me of God's faithfulness. In Genesis, Chapter 15, we learn of God's covenant with Abram (this is before his name was changed to Abraham). Abram says to the Lord, "*You have given me no children, so a servant in my household will be my heir.*" But in verse 4, the Lord said, "*This man will not be your heir, but a son coming from your own body will be your heir.*" He took him outside and said, "*Look up at the heavens and count the stars – if indeed you can count them.*" Then he said, "*So shall your off-spring be. Abram believed the Lord.*" How cool is that? God had just told Abram he will have as many descendants as there are stars in the sky. The amazing thing is Abram is old . . . way past child-bearing years, but when he is 100 and his wife is 90, she gives birth to their son, Isaac, even after they got impatient and schemed and took matters into their own hands. God was still faithful to them, and He is still faithful to us today. He never said life would be easy; in fact, the Bible tells us we will have trouble. But He promises to never leave us nor forsake us. (Deuteronomy 31:6)

By the way, do you know how many stars are estimated to be in the sky? At this writing the latest estimate from NASA shows that there are 100 thousand million stars in the Milky Way galaxy alone! That should lead us to worship!

That brings me to another thought this past week while on the trip. I've been feeling I'm almost at the end of my road; that my purpose in life is almost over since soon my girls will probably leave home to go away to college. I may be left all alone. This had not occurred to me before Brady left, as I figured we could do things together like travel. But as more time passes, my hope he wants to work things out is diminishing. I'm not saying I've lost hope in God, as God allows us our own free will and He may allow Brady to continue to drift and I not to follow. So, I'm in a holding pattern, which is really uncomfortable for me (I mean I plan my budgets six months in advance for heaven's sake!)

My minister, Rick, calls this place of not having answers a place of faith. So I'm going to work daily on knowing God is always with me, even and especially during trials. Lord, I pray no matter what happens, I can be a witness for You during this time. I figure no matter what path I'll be on, there could still be opportunities for me to help others.

Maybe I'll be used to help single moms, or maybe Brady and I together will work things out and be used to help re-build marriages in trouble. *Maybe I'll be used to house missionaries* when they visit the states. (Note: In January 2006, a young female missionary, named Gina, came to live with us for almost four years! I treasure those memories and she is now like a daughter to me.)

I don't know today where my journey will lead me and that is OK.

Lord, again thank You for the wonderful mission trip, the slowed down pace, the worship time, and the people who were with me.

III

A Song To Sing

On Thursday afternoon at the job site on our mission trip where we were installing floor tile in a house, I was especially feeling I was at a crossroads, that my life was in my husband's hands and control . . . and I hated that . . . I felt helpless. Our Youth Minister, Steve, who is also a friend, could tell I was struggling so he put down what he was working on and pulled me aside to talk. I told him how I was feeling, and he said the most amazing thing to me that I'll never forget: **"No matter what happens, God is still in control and you will still have a song to sing."** What he meant was for me not to worry . . . that really God is in control, not my husband; and no matter what path my life takes, whether the marriage is restored or whether my husband chooses to dissolve it, God still has a plan and purpose for me. Wow! See, I thought without my husband and when my girls are grown and out on their own, my purpose would be over. I was so wrong and my youth minister friend, Steve, was so right! Later I'll expand on this story, as it gets even better . . .

Tuesday, April 12, 2005

Today I listened to Chip Ingram on *Living On the Edge* radio show.[52] He was talking about being single and how we should look at it as a gift so we can focus more on God's desires and not have the added stress of a mate and children to please and care for. So I think I'm trying to prepare myself to be single.

Lord, if that is so, please be with me and help me to see it as a blessing and help me to truly learn to focus more on You – to have such an awesome love for you that I won't miss the love of a man. Maybe I've really never had that. Help me to focus on being the best person I can be, instead of looking for the best person I can find.

Lord, thank you for last week's mission trip experience. Thanks for allowing me to be a part of it. Help me to remember that each day is a part of my sojourn – the search for truth, my journey toward heaven. Help me be bolder for You. Amen.

Thursday, April 21, 2005

Today my counselor, Debbie, suggested I ask Brady if he has had an affair. She suggested maybe he is testing me to see if I'll fight for this marriage. Leaving me in a holding pattern is hurtful and in a way I am being shunned, which is a sort of abuse. Maybe this is all a cry for help. She said my top priority needs to be the goal of self-protection and to protect my girls. She suggested I write down questions to ask him and then to email him and ask for a meeting. I can ask him if he has a plan and where he is living. (I am his wife so I have a right to know!) I need to learn to deal with conflict so I need to start now by speaking up. I need to stand up for myself by being more assertive.

I am scared. I hate conflict. On one hand, he could say he wants to file for divorce and that would be so hurtful. On the other hand, he could want to meet and I'll cry right there in front of him. But maybe this is OK . . . it shows I'm hurting.

Monday, April 25, 2005

Today, I emailed Brady and asked for a meeting, as my counselor suggested. He emailed back and we set it up for Sunday at 3 p.m. I am nervous and scared already. I'm afraid I'll cry when I see him, but if I cry, I cry – there's nothing I can do about it. Either way, his answers will be tough. If he wants to end it, that will be hard because it means he really doesn't care about me enough to work on the marriage and our issues. But if that is what will happen, I might as well get on with it so I can get through it and quit having false hopes of restoration.

If he says he wants to work on it, that will be good but scary, too, because I'm not sure I trust him. So I've got people praying for me.

Lord, help me to be kind, but not a doormat. Help me to be strong if that is what I need to be. Help me to ask the right questions and help me to deal with the answers as You'd have me to. Lord, be with me and keep me from collapsing . . . or punching him. Help me to get through it in a way that would make you proud. If he wants to end this marriage, please be here for me as Your word promises. You know what it is like to be abandoned and rejected. Please give me a peace to know I'll get through it somehow. When I get lonely, help me to remember the Bible says that You'll be the father to the fatherless and a husband to the widow, but I hope you'll include me in there. If I'm to be single again, help me to be OK with that and to eventually even enjoy it. Help me to be a witness for You, Lord. Amen.

Friday, April 29, 2005

Today, I spoke with my counselor, Debbie, again. She agrees I need to meet with Brady on Sunday. She said I need to be strong, but kind, even godly. I truly hope I don't cry. I hope I can just see him and say, "Do you have a plan? This separation isn't healing or helping." I hope he'll be honest with me about a possible affair.

Lord, please help me to remember you are with me always so You will be with me. Please speak through me and help me to be strong and to stand up for myself. Help me to be able to handle any information he tells me in a way that would please You. Thank you for providing for my girls and me. Please protect us and our home another night. Thank you for my family and friends. Please keep me safe on Sunday, too. Amen.

The Meeting

Monday, May 2, 2005

I met with Brady yesterday at a public park after church. It was a beautiful sunny spring day. I took a deep breath as I got out of my car and saw him there. My voice quivered as I thanked him for meeting me. Then as we walked I asked, " So, do you have plan? This separation is not healing or healthy." He said, "Yes, I have a plan . . . actually I met with an attorney last week and I'm surprised you have not received divorce papers yet." What?! He was going to serve me with divorce papers without even letting me know! Coward! We continued to walk even though I was in a state of shock. Then I asked him if he'd had an affair. He said, "No." We walked a little more so I could ask him some more pointed questions about his plan to move out, and I'm pretty sure I even got up the nerve to call him an idiot at one point without caring if it hurt his feeling! (Looking back I'm not proud of that.) But I was crushed! He had never even mentioned divorce was an option and alluded to this separation as being a time when we both would work on ourselves. I assumed he was doing that. I asked him if he'd given up on God or just his church. He replied that he is tired of everyone else besides him giving half way. He explained he worked a fulltime job and then came and gave his time at church. I told him everyone does that – it's called volunteering! I didn't go on, as there was no point – he is so wrapped up in himself.

Since he'd decided divorce was what he wanted, there was really no point in talking or walking much more. I wasn't going to try to change his mind. I don't want to beg someone to stay married to me. (I already did that the day he left and it obviously had no effect.)

So the meeting lasted about 20 minutes. There was no point dragging it out. I don't think I even really looked at him — we both had sunglasses on so I didn't get to look into his eyes. I got into my car and drove off crying. It hurts to not be wanted anymore. It hurts to know my husband of almost nine years doesn't love me anymore. It hurts to be rejected by the person with whom I thought I'd spend the rest of my life. I am relieved he made this decision so my conscience is clear, but I hurt so badly. I know I have to heal and move on eventually, but right now, I just hurt. I went home, changed into sweats, curled up into a ball on my bed and cried my eyes out.

Wednesday, May 4, 2005

I guess at least I know which path my life will take and I know God will be right with me and He loves me. In Psalm 34:18, it says, "*blessed are the broken-hearted, they will be comforted.*" I will need some of that! I'll have to do some work to the house and probably sell it. Hopefully I can find or build a little house and start new. I also know I'll *eventually* have to forgive him because I am commanded to do so. I am so thankful for my job, as it will allow me to provide for my children. Thank You for the many people who love me.

Lord, please continue to keep my girls and me safe, and be with us each day. I need to pray for Brady, too. I pray for his parents and family, too. Lord, I'm sorry this marriage isn't working and I'm sorry for my part. Please forgive my shortcomings. Please help my heart to heal and to feel complete in You. Amen.

Sunday, May 15, 2005

A lot has happened this past week. Monday and Tuesday were really busy at work. On Wednesday, I went with my youngest brother, Jimmy, (the one who would beat someone up for me) who is also a real estate agent, and my girls to look at a condo. It was incredibly beautiful and even Nickie, my youngest daughter, who at first hated the idea of a condo because she has this unrealistic idea we'll get a big dog, loved it and was ready to move in. So we made an offer on Thursday, with a contingency that I'd sell the house, and it was accepted on Friday morning. However, apparently another person is interested in it, too, and if he wants it, the seller may ask me to drop the contingency paragraph. I love the condo, but have been praying for wisdom and God's will, so if this happens, I think this could be God shutting this door because He has something even better for me. It would not be wise to take the chance of possibly having two mortgage payments; plus legally, I don't know what is going to happen with the house.

Monday, May 17, 2005

I met with an attorney today. Before I went into her downtown office, I sat outside on a bench and cried. I tried to regain my composure, but I cried all through my meeting. She asked me, among other things, if I felt the marriage had been irretrievably broken and I had to answer honestly, "No," even though Brady had said "Yes" to this question. I left the same way I arrived, in tears, and could not go back to work. I went straight home and once again curled up on my bed and continued to sob for what felt like hours.

June 4, 2005

I have been so busy I can't believe it has been so long since I have journaled. Katie, my oldest daughter, graduated from high school last Friday, and we had her party on Saturday. We've also been getting the house ready to sell by installing new carpet, painting several rooms, and finally putting stone on the front of the garage. We listed it on Monday, May *23* and on Thursday, June 2, we got an offer. The offer is great and has no contingencies!

Lord, this must be from you. Since accepting the offer, we've had seven people call to look at it. Also, Sonya, the lady who owns the condo, never asked for me to drop the contingency! God, it looks as if this incredible grace is from You! You have given me a real estate agent, a painter, carpet installer, stone installer, boxes, packing materials and a buyer! So even though you hate divorce, you love me and are continuing to provide for me. What an awesome God you are!

June 13, 2005

It is still a busy time. It looks as though the girls and I will need to have everything in the house packed up and stored in the garage before we leave for vacation. (I had already planned and pre-paid for it, expecting it to be a family vacation for the four of us, but we might as well go and relax and enjoy it as much as we can. It will do us good to get away for a few days.) My realtor/youngest brother will overnight the closing documents to me for my signature, and I'll overnight them back. He will sign for me with Brady. On July 1, when I return from vacation, we'll move into the condo – our new home. How exciting . . . but also a little nerve-racking too. We've got a good amount of packing done already, but there is still much to do.

I still get sad at times, which is normal I am sure. I was married to Brady for almost nine years and saw him every day. I'm sad things didn't work out. I hate that holidays will be different – that I won't be with his family. I miss snuggling at night. I want to feel cherished and loved unconditionally, but God help me to remember that is exactly how You feel about me. I'm tired now and must get some sleep. Thank you, Lord for all the blessings, even the ones I unintentionally take for granted.

June 17, 2005

It's a Saturday morning, one week before we leave on vacation and then we will move. It will be our last week in this house. I obviously have mixed emotions. I'm really excited about the condo – it is beautiful and an obvious blessing from God! It really has my name written all over it. The red kitchen even matches my dishes! But, this has been our home for almost nine years, so it will be sad to leave – to realize this chapter of my life is coming to a close.

Lord, help me to be better about quiet time with you daily. I want to truly be close to You and be guided by You. Please help Brady to heal. He seems so angry. Lord, he needs You so I'll try to remember to pray for him more than I do. Please be with us today as we continue to pack up this house. Amen.

Wednesday, July 5, 2005

It's been quite a while since I've written. We've been busy finishing packing up the house, went to Tampa for a week, and then moved into the condo on Saturday, July 1. I guess I've been too busy to feel the hurt in my heart.

Vacation was nice but a couple of times it hit me that Brady was missing, especially when we'd go to a restaurant to eat and there'd be that empty fourth chair. And a couple of nights as I lay in bed by myself, I'd feel the loneliness and I'd quietly cry.

Why didn't things work out? Why couldn't we be happily married? I'm really sad tonight and I hurt. The condo is wonderful but it can't replace a mate who I thought loved me. Am I so unlovable? All I wanted was for Brady to be happy! I really tried, but obviously I failed. At the age of 40,

I'll be single again after another failed marriage. Lord, help me not to give up hope my life can be happy some day and my heart won't ache forever.

Monday, July 19, 2005

I've got to get better about journaling. I think sometimes I don't know what to say so I don't pray more. I try to remember to thank You, God, each day for the blessings You have given me. My counselor says it's OK to just hurt and cry and tell you, God, this is all I have to give at this time. I'm sort of there now, Lord.

Lord, I am truly sorry for my part in this broken marriage. My intentions were good – I truly wanted Brady to be happy. I worked full-time, cooked dinner almost every night (including a green vegetable per his request) did laundry, cleaned, paid the bills, balanced the checkbook, dropped off and picked up dry-cleaning, bought and wrote out cards and gifts, and took care of my daughters. Maybe I did too much, but I only did this because I thought it would make him happy.

They say hindsight is 20/20, and that is the case here. I thought my job as a wife was to be sure my husband was happy. That sounds pretty noble (and if any men are reading this they are probably shouting "Amen, Sister.") But the problem is my job as a wife was to be a helper, not a savior. No wonder I failed.

So if the goal is to help my husband be more like Christ, it is my responsibility to call him out on some action that is not helping with that. Of course this needs to be done in love. I've recently learned that wanting my husband to be happy at all costs unintentionally made him an idol to me.

I think I'm still sad about the death of the dream – the dream for a happy marriage. Maybe there really is no such thing for me.

Lord, help me to be content. I know it's normal to be sad and to grieve, but help me through this. When will the pain stop? Help me to find the strength to go to a divorce recovery class. I know I need to do this; it's just scary to go by myself and walk in the room. It's sort of publicly admitting I've failed. Lord, I hope this is not a pride issue. I don't mean to be proud; I just don't want people to think I'm a loser. (Maybe it is a pride issue!) Help me not to embrace this loser mentality. Thank you, God, for Your goodness, mercy, love, forgiveness and eternal life. Please watch over us again tonight and please keep us safe from harm. Amen.

IV

The Truth Is Revealed!

Well, what an enlightening week! Thankfully my bosses are gone on vacation, because I'm a wreck! I have got nothing accomplished at work and probably owe them! I prayed the Lord would help me to get past the sadness and grief of this broken marriage, and this week I found out the truth when I wasn't even looking for it! It's as if God was my private investigator but I didn't even know there needed to be an investigation!

On Tuesday, I received an email from one of Brady's co-workers that simply said, "If I were Brady's wife, I'd keep my eyes open. You are being played." I didn't reply, thinking this must be a mistake. A few days later I received another email from this same co-worker alleging several affairs. I could barely breathe. This hurts so much I can't even explain it, except that my heart literally hurts! It feels like I've been stabbed. And as I sob at my desk, I'm not even able to make a sound. This pain is too great for me to handle! When will it stop?! If this is true, my husband was not the man I believed him to be. I feel sick and can barely see. I trusted him with my whole heart! Who do I trust now?

So, I'm getting past the sadness all right – now I'm mad, again! I'm mad I've been crying over him for six months, when he's been lying about me and making me out to be a fool! Lord, I pray the Holy Spirit will give me the strength to not sin in my anger because right now I want to find him and punch his lights out!

I am shocked! I truly trusted him with my whole heart! Even after he left, I never suspected this from him! We even prayed at dinner as a family every night (including the night before he walked out) that "we'd live our lives in a way that would be pleasing to God." Hello?! I know I need to remember that "vengeance is mine sayeth the Lord" verse again right now because I am furious!

I want to confront him, and I've got the perfect scheme! I want to be able to strongly and boldly stand in front of him and let him know that I know the truth about him and his deceit-filled life. I want to tell him I am not stupid, except for trusting him . . . but isn't that what one is supposed to do in a marriage? I want him to hurt, as I have hurt for six months! I've been crying over him for six months!

Lord, I know I can't stay angry, so help me to get through this stage of the divorce and truly be able to put this behind me. Lord, please use me to be a witness for You, drawing others to You. That is the most important mission here – to let others know about You and Your love, grace, forgiveness and eternal life. Help me to be bolder about proclaiming You. Help me to stay pure, Lord, and to totally trust that You'll be with me. Your way is the only way to live a truly joy-filled life.

Lord, please help me to not try to find fulfillment in another man. After this blow, it is only natural to wonder if I am even attractive to anyone. Am I even worthy to be loved? Help me to truly find my worth, joy and completion in You. Lord, help me to always remember I am Yours, I am a reflection of You and this is my time to truly be a witness for You.

Lord, help me to remember I am Yours, so I am no loser. Lord, please protect us – keep angels watching over us as we travel to and from school, work, church etc. Thank You for my church family. Also help me to know Your will in regards to teaching high school Sunday school. Nickie has mentioned it, but I need to know Your will for me, so help me to know if this is what You want me to do.

I love You and thank You that even when anyone forsakes us, that You, the God of the universe, are right here for us – help me to always remember and claim Your promise that He who is in me is stronger than he who is in the world. Help me to remember You still have a plan for me and the rest of my life, and help me to be patient as I search for it. Amen.

Wednesday, July 27, 2005

Today was a better day. I told my brothers and my good friend, Mary, about the recent allegations. I had an enjoyable evening shopping with Mary for her honeymoon cruise. I truly pray for a wonderful marriage for her. Lord, help me to remember to take one day at a time (like you provided the manna for the Israelites) and help me to rest in You and to remember to be still and know that You are God. Tonight I've been listening to the CD of Building 429[3] and the words to a couple of their songs really hit me. I just kept singing them (no one else was home). One line says, "Your presence is always near." Wow, that is exactly how I feel. You have been with me so close lately and I thank You for Your timing of this latest information. Just like Mary expressed to me tonight, You knew I just would not have been able to handle this latest blow if it would have been exposed during the packing-up-the-house stage or before vacation.

Lord, help me to remember to stay out of Your way. Please continue to be with me and help me to heal and not become bitter and hate men and the idea of marriage. Help me refrain from becoming cynical and negative.

Debbie, my phone counselor, told me to read Mark 4:22. "*For whatever is hidden is meant to be disclosed, and whatever is concealed is meant to be brought out into the open.*" It means our sin will be found out eventually. And actually, as much as it hurts, that is probably best. It hopefully will make us confront it, learn from it, repent from it (which simply means to turn from it) and allows us to lead a new and even joy-filled life. I heard Kyle Idleman, the Teaching Minister from Southeast Christian Church say, "The only thing worse than having our sin found out, is not having it found out and living our life as a respectable fraud." I think he is right.

Thursday, July 28, 2005

Tonight after looking through photos, I hurt and cried again. My daughter, Katie, caught me crying. She came up and hugged me and said, "Mom, he's not worth your tears. In fact he's not even worth the booger you're gonna blow into that Kleenex!" How funny is that? For a moment, my tears of sorrow turned into tears of laughter. Bless her heart! What would I do without her?

I still can't believe the man I married changed so much. He was great during my dad's illness and death the week before our wedding. I don't understand what happened. How could he just stop loving me?

Lord, he really needs your guidance, so I'll go ahead and pray for him because he is one of Your children too. Thank You for the strength You have given me to get through this and to continue on working and being a mom. I'm sure I'll need some more of Your strength tomorrow, please.

Lord, help my girls to truly heal, too. I know there have to be truly godly men who will treat my girls as You would have it, so I pray for these young men right now. Thank You for Nickie's wisdom and for her reminder that I am being watched. I don't want to sin in my anger and ruin my reputation. I've said all along through this that I need to be a witness to others of Your incredible love and mercy and grace. Please help me with this.

A Divinely Appointed New Friend

Monday, August 1, 2005 10:35 am

Is God amazing or what? Today I received an email from Brady's first ex-wife, Whitney! My sister-in-law still keeps in touch with her, and she felt it might be helpful for both of us to communicate about our marriages to Brady. Whitney told me how she had been on her knees in prayer for me and my girls when she found out we were going to be married years ago, hoping my situation would be better than hers. We found out our marriages had a lot in common.

She shared with me how she blamed herself for his unhappiness in their marriage, as she didn't feel she was attractive enough and wasn't paying him enough attention due to a demanding job. Oh, how we women seem to blame ourselves for everything! After several conversations and emails, it has become clear we are so much alike. We even resemble each other (so her not being attractive enough was not the problem – Ha Ha). She has been so encouraging to me, reminding me that I am a child of God and He has an amazing plan for me. Our conversations have been healing for her, too. Even though she has been remarried for many years to a wonderful, godly man, at times she had questioned herself about her first marriage, if she had fought for it enough. But after finding out what happened in my marriage, it has been like God has erased any guilt she had. I love that God even erases our guilt! (Psalm 32:2).

Friday, August 5, 2005

Today has been sort of a tough day. I couldn't help but wonder if Brady ever really cared for me. Did he just marry me for stability, like I was informed he told a co-worker? Am I so unlovable? I've been abandoned by two husbands! What is wrong with me? I know I can't blame myself for *all* of this. My counselor said there is a spiritual battle going on and Satan is attacking men because they are to be the spiritual leaders in our homes, so when he gets them, marriages fail and families are torn apart. It's just like 2 Timothy: 3 says, "*they worm their way into homes and gain control over weak-willed women.*"

Lord, thank You for the truth. I know You have set me free, even though it still hurts. I truly loved him and I would have done anything for him. I pray for him now. I'm hurt. I'm still in disbelief. Thank You for the blessings of friends, family, job, my new home and my health. Amen.

August 9, 2005

"Who shall separate us from the love of Christ? Shall trouble or hardship or persecution or famine, or nakedness, or danger or sword? No, in all these things we are more than conquerors through Him who loved us. For I am convinced that neither death nor life, neither angels nor demons, neither the present nor the future, nor any powers, neither height nor depth, nor anything else in all creation, will be able to separate us from the love of God that is in Christ Jesus our Lord." Romans 8:35; 37 – 39. I love that verse!

Today the SECC Worklife Ministry sent out the following message:

"Sometimes, life is not about moving forward. **Sometimes the struggles we face are simply so overwhelming it takes all the strength we have merely to hold on**." The article went on to talk about a missionary couple whose daughter and son died quickly of Scarlet Fever in 1904. To escape the disease, the mother and three remaining children boarded a train to return to the states, while the father stayed behind to bury the two children who had died. Before the train reached home, the other three children also died of the fever. In a letter the father sent to the Foreign Mission Board, he wrote, "sometimes it seems more than we can bear . . ."

The article continued, "Some of you are facing just such a time right now. The pain of the loss of a loved one, the loss of a job, the debilitating and misunderstood darkness of depression; all of these and so much more are real parts of a fallen world. In these moments, it often seems more than we can bear. We cry out to God with questions, sometimes even in frustration and anger. When the answers aren't apparent, it often feels like He isn't there, or isn't listening. He is there and He is not silent, though the sound of His voice may be hard to discern and the touch of His hand may not be easily felt. These are the times when the work of the Holy Spirit goes on in you even in fits of rebellion, even in the very face of spiritual doubt. When you can no longer pray, the Holy Spirit lifts your heart's deepest prayer for you." Romans 8:26

I have been there! I have come home from making it through another day of work, and fell by my bed to my knees in exhaustion and tears. Not necessarily physical exhaustion, but emotional exhaustion. Sometimes I couldn't even pray. I didn't even know what to pray. All I could do was cry because the pain of being rejected (again) was so great. But I believe God saw me, His child, and even though I couldn't pray, He knew what I needed even more than I did, and somehow, miraculously, I would have a peace that I can't explain. He gave me a peace of knowing even though I couldn't see Him or hear Him, that He was there in my heart and He cared. No, nothing can separate us from the love of God. Praise Him!

I have recently learned the most amazing thing from Beth Moore's "A Woman's Heart God's Dwelling Place" Bible Study[3]. She said Jesus is at the right hand of God interceding for us! (Hebrews 7:25) What an amazing picture to me. Jesus is waiting for my prayers so that He can tell them to God! Thank you, Lord!

August 13, 2005 11:35 p.m.

Tonight, both girls were gone. I was alone at home and too tired to clean anymore so I just read a book. I felt lonely. I should be used to that, as the last several years of the marriage, Brady was hardly ever home on Saturday nights, so I'm surprised this bothered me. Talking to Whitney last night made me feel so much better, because unlike most of my other friends, who are so supportive, she's been through it. I told her how I can't help but wonder, wasn't I worth his time, honesty, kindness and love? Will I ever feel cherished? Will I ever get to be someone's very best friend – the one someone immediately thinks of when he has a story to tell or exciting news to share? Will there ever be a man who will be crazy about me and think I'm beautiful, smart and fun to be with and worthy of a proposal on one knee . . . someone who will want to spend the rest of his life with me?

Last week I read a devotional about the desires of our heart – about listening and consulting them. Psalm 37:4 "*Take delight in the Lord and He will give you the desires of your heart.*" God knows this desire of mine to be truly cherished, so Lord, help me to be patient and to know it is not time; I need to finish grieving and heal. I know until I have healed completely, I have nothing to bring to a relationship. So, the most important thing for me to focus on is how I can serve God, and know to the core of my being that He does cherish me.

Lord, I pray for my daughters. Help them to heal and to get rid of any malice. Please help them to be strong and to stand for Godly principles. I pray now for their future spouses, if that is Your plan for them, that they will be authentic in their faith and will treat my girls with the respect, love and the honor they deserve. Thank You for my church family, my friends and family. They have been great. Thank You for my new friend, Whitney, and for her willingness to talk to me. Thank You that she has moved on and is happily married and has two children – blessings from You. Please continue to get me through each day. Thank You for the strength You have already given to me so far. I love the line in Chris Tomlin's song, entitled, Holy is the Lord, where it says, "The joy of the Lord is our strength."[4] *(Now that I think of it, I think that is straight from the Bible, too!)*

Thursday, August 25, 2005

Today I talked to Debbie, my phone counselor, and she said the following:

1) Narcissistic men usually choose women who become dependent upon them, so they can be the hero. My first reaction was that that is not me; I'm pretty independent, but thinking back to when I met my husband, that wasn't quite the case. I was a young single mom living paycheck to paycheck, so he probably saw us as needy. But, when my income increased past his, maybe that made him feel less needed. It seems we wanted different things from the marriage. I wanted love while he wanted power, and to him money was power. These rarely mix, according to Debbie.
2) She wants to be sure the girls and I don't become bitter and hate men and marriage. She said that we have to look for "fruits" from people to see what they are really made of and what they truly believe. This takes time.
3) She suggested I read Beth Moore's book entitled, "When Godly People Do Ungodly Things".[5]

A Promise

Sunday, August 28, 2005

Today, I received an email from Greg, a friend I haven't seen in about eight years. He and his wife had heard of the divorce and were astounded and hurt for me. I actually grew up with his wife and she ended up going to high school and rooming with Whitney in college, and he was a roommate of Brady's in college. So after Brady and Whitney's divorce, they lost contact with Whitney, just assuming that she was at fault. He encouraged me to read Job 42 and to pay attention to verse 12. So I did. It says, "*The Lord blessed the later part of his life more than the rest.*" Wow – I don't remember reading that before. Now that is a promise for me! I also love verse 2 where Job says to God, "*I know that you can do all things; no plan of Yours can be thwarted.*" What incredible faith! This man had lost all he had, including his children, his wealth and his health (I mean the guy was in such torment he was scratching himself with broken pottery, for Pete's sake) but he still had no doubt God had a plan for him. What a role model for me.

I cried in church today . . . again. It still hurts so much to know my husband didn't think I was worth staying married to. The day he left, he said I was a great wife. So why then did he leave? Why wasn't he willing to work things out? Looking back, I can't help but wonder if God actually removed him from our home so I could find out the truth, grieve, heal and move on with my life . . . the abundant life God has for me.

Lord, thank You for getting me through each day. Thank you for Greg's email – perfect timing – as I'd forgotten about this verse in

Job. How reassuring to know my future will be blessed by You because You know me and my heart, and You know I truly want to live a life pleasing to You. I want to hear someday from You, "Well done, good and faithful servant."

Wednesday, August 31, 2005

Today, I just haven't felt that well so I just watched the continuous coverage of the devastation of Hurricane Katrina on TV. I am in disbelief. This is heart breaking. Lord, please be with these people, the leaders, the relief workers, police, etc. Somehow I pray that Your name will be glorified. I pray that your church will come through and show the love of Christ to these people.

After watching this, my problems seem so small and I feel a little selfish and self-absorbed. Seems like I shouldn't be praying for me at all, but only for those folks affected by this hurricane. But I know my God hears all prayers and He can handle them all.

Thursday, September 1, 2005

Today I received an email from Whitney. She told me she has been praying for me and she has been thanking God she has gotten to know me. She said she feels so much more whole after being able to share her story with me; that this has actually been healing for her too! God, You are amazing! Also, she and Greg & Lisa have gotten back in touch after all these years, and they are going to schedule a visit soon! Once again, God, You show Your awesomeness! Thank You for allowing me to be a tiny part of the restoration of this relationship.

I talked with my counselor today, and she reminded me it is important to accept my singleness and to pray for contentment and for knowledge of where God wants me to be. She explained it is normal for a woman to desire to have a man of her own, as God designed us that way. In Genesis 3:16, God said to Eve, ". . . *Your desire will be for your husband* . . ." (the next line says that "*he will rule over her,*" but let's not go there).

She also explained that in order to be wise when (and if) the time for me to start dating comes around, I need to be whole so I won't foolishly attract men who will want to be "the big cheese."

She reminded me of Isaiah 40:10, "*See, the Sovereign Lord comes with power, and His arm rules for Him. See, His reward is with him, and His recompense accompanies him. He tends His flock like a shepherd: He gathers the lambs in his arms and carries them close to His heart; He gently leads those that have young.*"

Brady always wanted to be admired. I can't help but wonder if when I started earning more income than he, if he felt threatened. Maybe he thought I was the one with the power in the relationship, and I wouldn't respect him any longer. I would have never thought that! I was excited for this blessing and truly considered it our money. I can't help but wonder about a time in December, and even in early January, when a couple of the middle school girls in my small group were baptized and I was recognized in church as an influence on them, if this bothered him too. When people would compliment me after singing, or when I received praise for a job well done at work, did that also bother him? Did Whitney's public job bother him? I don't understand why he couldn't just be proud of us.

Lord, if I did anything wrong to cause this marriage to die, even unintentionally, I apologize and beg Your forgiveness. I believe You know my heart and that I truly loved Brady and only wanted the best for him. I will try to remember to pray for him more.

Please help me to be content with being single, to grow and totally trust You with my future, as I know You want only the best for me. I love Jeremiah 29:11, "For I know the plans I have for you, declares the Lord, plans to prosper you and not to harm you, plans to give you hope and a future." Amen!

Lord, help me to do the best I can as a Sunday school teacher. I believe it is what You want me to do, so please be with me, and allow the kids to really enjoy it but to learn too. Help me to be genuine. Please shine through me to them.

Thursday, September 15, 2005

I was having a good day, even received an email from Whitney which I've been getting almost every day for the last several weeks. I really enjoy hearing from her. It has been so healing for me to know someone who has been in my shoes and has not only survived, but is thriving.

Tonight was parent open house at the high school and I'm really glad I went, but I saw an old friend and told her about what had happened. In the parking lot on the way to the car, I teared up. There were so many couples there and it is hard for me to see that. Debbie told me that I will probably have some more sad feelings come to the surface during the divorce recovery class, so to just be aware of that. It is completely normal and part of the healing process.

Lord, I really want to heal and I want to do Your will, so help me to know what that is. Thank You for the many blessings You have given me. You have been so evident through all of this – so help me to be a witness for You.

Saturday, September 25, 2005

I wrote an email to a friend today who is going to attend a new church. I know it sometimes can feel weird going to a new place, but I think God wants us out of our comfort zones at times so we have to trust in Him and not in ourselves. This is exactly how I feel about teaching the Junior/ Senior Sunday School class! But I read the most amazing thing in a book I picked up yesterday that said, "*Competence is not one of the fruits of the spirit.*"[6] I'd never thought of that before – how liberating! The funny thing is that just last night when I prayed before dinner, one of my prayers was that I'd do a good job teaching this class, that it wouldn't be a waste of an hour that the teens hated. I feel so inept at teaching, but I just love the kids, so that is why I offered to do it. I am praying God will use that love to reach them and overlook my lack of teaching ability. The book is written by Christian recording artist Chris Tomlin. He is one of my favorite artists, as the lyrics in his songs are so powerful. The book is about how God has been working in his life and how some of his worship songs came about.

Also, it gave me additional hope that if God has a guy out there for me someday, that there really are some who are truly committed to Him. In the book, Tomlin touched on the verse about "God knowing the desires of our hearts." You know, when I really think about it, I really do desire to be married again some day but I desire a real marriage . . . not a mirage. I want one that will truly and totally honor God! I know I am not ready now, as I really want to heal completely and use this time to focus on God's will for me. I have mixed emotions. Within the next few years, Katie and Nickie will be away at school. One part of my heart hurts to think about this, to think they'll be out on their own, not needing me anymore, but the other part of my heart says, "Look out, if I really do take time to just be still and concentrate on what God wants for the rest of my life, what a journey could be in store." I am so thankful for the hope I have!

Sunday, September 26, 2005

Today I heard a great message at church about being holy. My minister explained this only comes from Christ living in me, and I should pray daily that I will reflect the light of Christ living in me. My minister also said that busy-ness at church isn't holiness. When we truly love God and our neighbors, we can then be holy. We are called to be eccentric, which actually means "off-center." Wow – unlike the world tells us – we are not to be selfish and have our-selves as the center of our world – we are to have Christ as the center of our world. I read the entire Chris Tomlin book last night! It was so incredible and I got so much out of it. His love for God and his desire to truly please Him is so evident throughout the book, and that is exactly what I wish for in a future spouse, if that is God's will for me. (I think I have a little crush!)

Another cool thing in the book was Tomlin spoke of several meanings when we raise our hands. One was the example of how a toddler holds his hands up when he wants to be held. Well, a blind man at church today, who normally does not sit on "my side" of church, sat a few rows in front of me. At one point during one of the worship songs, he just reached his hands up as far as he could. Tears came to my eyes, and I actually had to stop singing as I watched this beautiful, unbridled attitude of total surrender to God. Oh, to be more like him!

Oh God, help me to heal and become whole with You in my heart and with my desire for You to be glorified in my life. Help me to wake up with the attitude of wanting to let Your light shine in me. Thank You for leading me to Tomlin's book and thank You for the author's desire and follow-through in writing it. Thanks for his heart for You. I pray that You have a truly Christian man whose heart is for You for me some day. Help me to totally trust You and to remember to be still and listen for You.

Thank you for my family, friends, church and job. Thank you for loving me as you do – as Your child. Thank you, Jesus for your sacrifice for me. Amen.

V

Seeking

Monday, September 27, 2005

Just yesterday, I was telling Whitney how I believe God had **removed** Brady from my life. I think God knew I would hurt and grieve, but maybe He just could not stand by and watch my false marriage continue with me not knowing what was really going on. Proverbs 10:30 says, *"The righteous will never be uprooted, but the wicked will not remain in the land."* I also told her how important it is to encourage our husbands to be involved in church and in God's Word; I did not pressure Brady at all to attend church with me the last few years of the marriage. Although I would never want to re-live any of my past, I have more peace in my heart today than ever. It's as if God physically removed Brady from my life so I could find out the truth, go through it, learn from it, work on healing, and then move on and serve Him with my whole heart and life. I was serving in church and serving my family the best I knew how, but I always had some fear in the back of my mind that Brady would either be mad at me or in a bad mood. So now I can take this energy and use it to focus more on God, where the only fear is the healthy fear of knowing He is the all-powerful Savior who holds our lives in his hands.

Lord, thank You for the blessings You pour out on me and forgive me when I seem ungrateful. You truly amaze me with all You've done for me and will continue to do. I love You so, Lord, and thank you for giving me the truth, even though I know it grieved You to see me hurting. You knew I'd grow stronger and closer to You. Help me to truly be a witness of Your love and mercy and grace. Lord, I am full with a thankful heart tonight. I have so many wonderful friends and family members who love me and pray for me constantly.

Today I received a narrative called *A Heavenly Strategic Planning Session from the Southeast Worklife Resources.* Could this be a God-incident? Here is a portion of it. "If God wanted to use you to impact your world for Jesus Christ, what circumstances would have to be created in order for you to respond to His call? What would your response be, should God and the angels conclude the only way to move you into a position of fulfilling God's purpose was to **remove** some things that might be very dear to you? There are many examples of God bringing major upheaval in the lives of those He called for His purposes. Why? **The reason is that we do not seek God with a whole heart in time of prosperity and comfort. Prosperity and comfort tend to breed complacency and satisfaction. It is rare to find a man or woman who seeks God with a whole heart who does so simply from a grateful heart. We often must have pain or crises to motivate us**. Eventually, that crisis bridges us to a new calling, and we embrace that calling if we are open to the Holy Spirit's work in us. We can actually thank God for the change that was required to get us to this place, but it is not without anguish of heart. Ask God to give you the grace and trust in His love for you to say 'yes'." Amazing timing for sure!

Thursday, September 29, 2005

This morning when I woke up, my first conscience thought was "the truth will set you free." Then in the shower I found myself singing the words to a Chris Tomlin song that included the lyrics "*I am loved by the Father, I am loved by the Son, It is love that has captured the heart of this wayward one.*"[7] So I thought of Brady. But before I think too highly of myself, I need to remember that in just a heartbeat, I too could be the wayward one if I do not focus daily on Christ and on serving and pleasing Him.

So tonight, Lord, I pray for Brady – I don't know what he is doing or who he may be with, but he has to be hurting. I pray that somehow he will draw close to You and truly live a joy-filled life. This has got to be the Holy Spirit in me because my fleshly desire is for justice. I'm working on forgiving – giving up my right to retaliate, as my mom defines it. Besides, I've heard it said we are most like God when we forgive, and that is my whole goal in life – to be more like God. Believe me, I have a long way to go, but it is an incredible goal. Please be with his family and help them to be kind to him and full of mercy and forgiveness, and help him to heal.

Sunday, October 2, 2005

Today, Sunday school class went well, but this week I want to start on my lesson earlier so I can really be prepared.

I truly desire for the kids to enjoy the class and not think it is a waste of their time.

Lord, help me with this please, as I am definitely out of my comfort zone. Please use me to teach them.

Also today, I thought about how I need to start working out. I mean I want to look good in case I meet the man You have for me, but help me to remember that although working out is a worthy goal, I need to mainly desire to take care of my body as it is a temple for You, so You should be the One I am trying to please. You need to be the reason I get in shape and stay healthy. Maybe I never thought about it, or maybe I just assumed that You'd be pleased if I was in OK shape as You love me already so I don't have to work on "luring" You in. Not that I desire to trap a man; it's just that You made them in a way where the physical appearance does get their attention and I want to be as good as I can be to get the attention of the one You have chosen for me, if that is Your plan. If that isn't, help me to be more than content with my singleness and to also (no matter what) be on the lookout for Your plan for my life to witness to others . . . and when necessary, as St Francis of Assisi said, "use words." Amen.

Sunday, October 9, 2005

Sunday school went well this morning. Our Youth Minister, Steve, taught with me, and he did a great job talking about the Jewish traditions and Jesus as a teenager. I don't teach for 2 weeks since I'm returning to the vocal team. This will be the first time since January, so I'm looking forward to it. But I am a little nervous, hoping I don't get emotional and cry in front of the whole church. I found myself getting a little emotional today in church thinking about Katie leaving for college soon and then realizing that Nickie is not far behind her. This afternoon at home alone,

I found myself a little mad at Brady for leaving me at this time in my life, knowing that soon, I'll probably be all alone.

Lord, again, help me to trust You – that You'll not only get me through the girls leaving, but that You'll help me to thrive – not get depressed and stay all to myself but figure out what You want me to do with my time. Surely there is something I can do for You! Please help me to enjoy the next few months with both of my girls at home. I'm sure it is normal to get emotional. Help me to be confident when it is time to do "single" things (yuck) and not rush into any relationship. I know that right now I am not ready. (Holey cow, I'm not even divorced yet!) I truly want to heal and become the whole person You have made me to be. Maybe I'll even learn to play the piano or guitar, paint or take gourmet cooking classes, or even tennis lessons (if it does not require sporting one of those short tennis skirts). Lord, please keep us safe, and keep Katie, Nickie and me close to Your heart. Amen

Monday, October 16, 2005

Yesterday, I returned to the vocal team from my sabbatical, and I truly enjoyed it. PJ, our music minister, told me it was so good to have me back. Several other people said so too, and that made me feel so special. Thank you, Lord for my incredible church family! I also saw an attractive man at church sitting by himself. Maybe his wife was at home sick or maybe she was working in the nursery. I wasn't close enough to see a wedding ring, but either way, maybe this is a sign that I am healing since I noticed an attractive guy and was not turned off by the whole gender!

My phone counselor, Debbie, has told me I should wait at least 9 months after the divorce is final before I start dating – so that will probably be around next August. I expect the divorce to be final in November. So, Lord, help me to be wise and patient and to be in touch with Your will and perfect timing for me. (Side note – as I get this book ready to publish, it has been 8 years since my husband left and I have only gone out with one guy three times, 5 years ago – and I have more than survived! Funny. So **don't rush the whole dating thing**!)

Wednesday, October 19, 2005

Tonight I had dinner with Angela, my accountant friend, and we had a great time as usual. She suggested I eventually try the dating website, e-harmony.com. She took the self-evaluation and said it really made her look at herself and learn about herself, so maybe eventually I'll try that. I need to remember to be patient and to work on healing totally and to figure out who I am before I get into the dating world. I need to discover what my desires or gifts are (as most of these are probably God-given) and what I think God wants me to do with this new fresh-start He has given to me. Lord, help me to be wise.

Lord, if you do have a partner out there for me some day, help me to not worship him or any man, the created, rather than You, the Creator! Help me not take for granted for one second the incredible invitation to pray and spend time with You. Help me to remember that I am "only one step away from being off track," as my friend Christy said. Help me to never think more highly of myself than I should. Thank You for loving me. Amen.

Saturday, October 22, 2005

Last night some friends came over for dinner and we had a great time. I asked one of them how she got past the shame of having gone through two divorces, and she said it takes time and prayer. She reminded me of the verse that says, "*There is no condemnation for those in Christ Jesus.*" (Romans 8:1) She explained that if we don't believe this then we don't believe that Christ's death was enough of a sacrifice. Wow – I'd not thought of it that way. I need to remember this every day when that shame wants to rear its ugly head.

Lord, thank you for my friends. You just continue to amaze me. It is hard to imagine that You, God, can be so concerned about me and my life when there are billions of other people in the world. You truly are bigger than I can even begin to fathom!

Lord, I want to glorify You with my life, so please lead me each day. I need to remember that You may have me serve in an ordinary way, or You may have me serve in an extraordinary way. Whichever it is, help me to find it and to delight in it. I know that Your plan is better than anything I can come up with, so please help me focus on the good and keep me pure and thinking on those things that are good. Please be with all who have fallen and I pray they will seek You and Your forgiveness.

Monday, October 24, 2005

Last night before I fell asleep, I found myself day-dreaming about having a husband who would actually cherish me. As a teenager, I had low self-esteem and latched onto the first guy who gave me any attention. I was sure no one else would find me attractive and my whole goal in life was to get married, have children and live happily ever after. Yep, I wanted the fairytale. I think even as a little girl, I dreamed of being cherished or feeling like I was pretty and special. Now, in hindsight, I know my dad loved me like crazy, but he just didn't express it in a way I understood at that time.

I didn't know what true unconditional love was; or so I thought. I was under the impression I had to earn someone's love, and this is pretty scary, because if you have to earn it, you could also lose it. I remember during my teenage years, comparing myself to my friends who were taller or thinner or more talented, and was sure my dad would have preferred to have one of them as his daughter instead of me, who was a short tomboy. Years later when I was in my thirties, I remember talking with my dad and saying I bet he wished one of my cousins, who is a beautiful dentist, was his child instead of me, and he about wrecked the car. I think he was shocked at my statement. He told me he loved his kids so much! And he didn't care what their profession was. Whatever we chose to do, he wanted us to do well and he was proud of each of us. Wow. I wish I would have had this conversation with him years ago, but I am glad he was able to clear up my misconception.

Lord, You are my Abba Father and I thank You that there is no misconception about Your unconditional love for me. I want You to be the love of my life now and forever, and I want to be able to know Your perfect will for the rest of my life. Holy Spirit, please replenish me daily and help me to think on things from above.

Friday, October 21, 2005

Today, I sent an email to Steve, our Youth Minister, thanking him for finding a sub to teach my Sunday school class so that I could be on vocal team last Sunday. He responded with, "God gave you a *song to sing* and a beautiful voice to sing it with, so it is only natural that it would be fulfilling to use it for His glory in that way." What a nice response. It was similar to what he told me during the Spring

Break trip to Mexico when I was having a tough day feeling I was in a holding pattern, not knowing what was going to be the ultimate outcome of my marriage. I remember Steve telling me that no matter what happens, I will still have a "song to sing." No matter what happens, God would still use me and my life to glorify Him. I love that!

Then tonight when I was getting ready for my quiet time, I opened Chris Tomlin's book, and just happened to open to page 133, which just happens to be entitled, "The Song In You." I cracked up! How cool is that? God, are you smiling down at me or what? (I can almost imagine a grin on His face.) In this chapter, he talks about "the song in you," meaning a passion or unique ability that seems to have God's signature on it in your life." He goes on to say, "Maybe you are sensing God moving you in a certain direction in your life, but you have no idea how to make that happen."[8]

Hello, that is exactly how I feel about the book I am writing! I've told my friends that if God allows me to publish my work, it will definitely be from Him, as I am not an author and I have no idea what the next steps are. I only know I feel a desire deep in my heart to use my experiences to encourage others, and to give them hope for their future by telling of God's provision and peace He has blessed me with and wants to bless them with, too. Tomlin's book says more about this, but instead of quoting it, you should just get a copy and read it yourself. It will bless you.

Thursday, October 27, 2005

Today was a difficult day for me. Last night at church after vocal team practice, someone asked me if I'd heard from Brady lately. I maintained my composure but was surprised by this question and sort of felt like I'd been punched in the stomach. I simply replied I had not heard from him in months except for him filing for divorce. He was shocked and felt bad for asking, so I told him, "Please don't feel bad about asking. I know it is an uncomfortable situation, so just pray for him." Since that conversation, my mood went down hill. I came home and ate ice cream right out of the carton and was a little grouchy. It just brought up the hurt all over again, and I know I'll have to go through the same sort of questions many more times.

Today I cried when I talked to my counselor. She assured me my feelings were normal and I will have good days and tough days ahead. She is glad I am exercising, involved in church and spending time with my friends, so I am not isolating myself and falling into a deep depression. She also suggested that Gina (a young missionary friend) possibly moving in with us could be a "God thing," as Nickie and I may not be ready to experience another "loss," so she'll fill the void that Katie will leave when she goes away to school in Cincinnati. (Not that Katie is replaceable, because if you knew her, you'd know that is definitely not true.)

I also realize if I met someone now, it would be too soon, as I'd be unconsciously looking to him to fix my broken heart and that would just be a temporary fix. I know I need to remain in God's word and to truly allow Him to heal me and make me whole before I have anything to offer anyone. I want also to search and find His perfect plan for me. I am hoping His plan includes a truly wonderful Christian man whose heart is to honor God with his life. And I wonder if this desire wasn't put in my heart by my Creator himself? So my goal is to be in God's word daily and desire to know Him more; and to make Him the love of my life.

Lord, please be with me and keep me from temptations. I want to have a pure heart for You. Please reveal Your plan for me, Lord, and help me be the best I can be. Thank You for being with me this tough year and for the evidence of your fingerprints on this situation, especially with the re-connection of Whitney with Greg and Lisa after all these years. It is so like You to bring about healing from a hurt-filled situation! Only You can bring "beauty from ashes," which was my friend, Mary's, prayer for me in January after Brady left. Thank You for loving me like You do, and for providing for my girls and me. I do feel You have big plans for me and I'm excited to know what they are.

Saturday, November 5, 2005

Yesterday I went to Chicago with Nickie's business class and we had a great time. It is a big bustling city, which is not what I am used to, but I really liked visiting there. A couple of times I felt a little lonely as I saw couples shopping together (men even accompanied their wives in boutique-like stores). I still can't help my desire to be cherished by a truly Godly man. Again, maybe this desire is from God so I'm not giving up hope on it. I also am reminded I cannot lose the truth . . . that God the Creator of all does cherish me . . . now, just as I am, without waiting for me to lose weight or tone my arms. Just as I am! I know I need to continue to strive to be more like Christ (compassionate, forgiving, faithful, kind, giving) so Lord, help me to remember that. This is my most important goal.

Sunday, November 5, 2005 10:45 pm

I was reminded today in church how important it is to have a heart of gratitude. I want to be sure to be like the one leper who returned to thank Christ for his healing.

Lord, Lenisa (one of my dear friends) and I leave this week for Orlando for the Women Of Faith conference. Please keep us safe as we travel and bless our time together. Thank You for our friendship. (See, I'm a quick learner.) Please be with the speakers and allow them to touch hearts and plant seeds. Thank You for each of these women and for giving them the courage to share their experiences and give hope of healing to thousands of women each year. Thank You for using their weaknesses to glorify You. I can't help but wonder what You have in store for me. Thank You for the many blessings You have given me, including my senses and the ability to walk and talk and hear and sing – how I love to do that! *Thank You that our song was so well received last week at church. I hope it brought pleasure to Your ears.*

Lord, please be with me through this divorce process, as I just want it to be over. I pray for Brady – that he'll lead a good life for You. Help me to totally forgive him, as You command me to do. Please forgive me when I fail You.

Sunday, November 13, 2005

Wow! The Women Of Faith conference was the best! The pre-conference especially spoke to me. I jotted down some notes so I could refer back to them. Recording artist, Kathy Troccoli spoke on being single and content, but said she does have days when she thinks it would be great if God sent her a man to share her life with. She clings to the scripture that God will be the father to the fatherless and a husband to the husbandless.

Marilyn Meberg spoke about God allowing bad things to happen because He gives us free will to choose good or bad. Sometimes we are affected negatively by someone else's bad choices, but ultimately, God's plan will still work out. She also spoke about having joy in our life and it is physically good for us to laugh! It exercises the liver!

Sheila Walsh's main theme was that God is in control no matter what is going on in our lives – we can know the truth – God is in control today.

Pasty Clairmont's main point was: don't go too fast and don't panic. She said not to move too quickly through the valley in life – to be sure to learn all that God wants to teach you while you are there. So this is my prayer – that I will be still and let God teach me His will for my life and be still before Him and learn.

Thelma Wells encouraged us to **know** we are forgiven. She quoted Romans 8, "*There is no condemnation for those who are in Christ*"! (Sounds familiar!)

Luci Swindoll talked about the faith of her father, grandfather and brothers. She said we need to be sure we are passing faith on to our children.

Lord, what an incredible weekend. I thank You for the privilege of attending. I had tears running down my cheeks at one time on Friday because I was so touched. Lord, please allow me to remember all these truths I've written down, in my heart and in my mind. May I focus on Your will, whatever it is. I want to pursue writing a book to help others through divorce and to show Your hand in my life, especially during this "valley".

Monday, November 21, 2005

Yesterday I was very emotional. At church I had tears running down my face pretty much during the entire service. I don't think I missed Brady, but I still hurt, I still feel abandoned, confused, and a little lonely. I'm sure with the holidays coming up, these feelings are normal. I am not sure what I'll do on Thanksgiving day. I've had several invitations, but I may just stay by myself and enjoy some solitude. I might read and maybe even write some remembering all God has done for me. When Katie and Nickie get home from their dad's, we can set up the Christmas tree and decorations. Maybe this is part of the healing process – being OK alone (but not totally alone because God will never leave me) so we'll see.

Last night, I went to my first small group, and it was great. I was invited a couple of weeks ago by Stan and Barbara, the small group leaders, who attend my church. I politely thanked them for the invitation when they phoned, and told them I'd pray about it, but what I really meant was "no." I almost didn't go since I'd been emotional and didn't want to cry in front of people I didn't even know, but at the last moment, decided to give it a shot. I was close to crying a couple of times, but didn't, thankfully. The book we are studying is about having true faith in Christ, as when Peter stepped out of the boat and walked on water. This will be a great lesson for me during my "valley" time.

Lord, I do feel You have a purpose for me and will reveal it to me when You are ready. Help me in the meantime to work on healing, draw closer to You, and enjoy each day of my life as part of my journey. I don't want to miss a thing!

(Note: I have been part of this small group for almost 7 years now, and it has been a blessing! I would encourage you to join one. There is nothing like having a group of people who know you – the good, bad and ugly – and love you anyway. We have laughed together (a lot), cried together, attended weddings and baby showers together, shared our hurts and pains, and continue to draw closer to God together. I believe we are created to live in community, so really, you've got to get involved in one. My life would not be complete without this group of friends, who are really now like family to me.)

God, You are awesome and mighty and greater than I can even fathom! Yet You love me and have time to listen to my heart and prayers. Your hand is on my life, I know! I desire to walk so close to You, Lord, that I can feel Your arm and shoulder rub mine. The Savior of all whose name is above all names wants that close walk with me, a sinner . . . a single mom with two divorces under her belt, but who has a moldable heart and life that I offer Him to use for His glory.

November 26, 2005

Today has been tough. I received a call from my attorney saying she has received a copy of the divorce decree and would send me my copy. Probably tomorrow, the 10th anniversary of our first date, I will receive my divorce papers in the mail. I believe I did all I could do to save the marriage, and God freed me totally, but it still hurts so much. I have this desire to be cherished; I trusted this man to do that for the rest of my life, and he just decided not to anymore. I know I am cherished by my Heavenly Father, and that should be more than enough. That needs to be my goal – to totally focus on how much God cherishes me – enough to die for me! Amazing!

Lord I apologize for wanting more. What is wrong with me? You are the Creator and You love me so much. Help me to focus on that and be satisfied in You.

November 27, 2005

Today is exactly 10 months from the day Brady walked out. In the mail was my divorce decree. So it is officially over. I opened the envelope, saw his signature, and cried like a baby. I knew it was going to happen, but it still hurts so badly! It's not so much I miss him anymore, but I still have a hard time believing he didn't think I was worth fighting for. But I guess for him, it was really over a couple years ago. I know it is normal to feel this way and it is OK to hurt and cry. I know it is actually part of the healing process.

Lord, I really want to totally heal and to learn all that You have for me during this time.

December 8, 2005

Today I received an email from Whitney and she wrote the most interesting sentence: "Maybe God wants you all to himself right now and He is preparing you for great things and great relationships." Wow, never thought of that! That the Creator could want *me* to Himself? How blessed and humbled am I?

Oh Lord, forgive me when I want more – I truly want to mean the words "You are more than enough for me" when I sing them at church or along with the radio or CD. It is amazing that You still love me even when I have blemishes on my face or when all I have to give You is my tears.

December 10, 2005

Today I cried several times. I felt the hurt all over again. I hope I can truly enjoy Christmas with my family and not be sad. At least this year Brady isn't continuing to string me along and pretend he cares for me. At least I know the truth and the truth sets me free – indeed it has – it just hurts after being with someone for almost nine years of my life. Even though I was stressed, lonely and unhappy at times, I just figured we would work through it. I would not have left him – I meant 'til death do us part.

So Lord, today I just have the broken pieces of my life and heart to lay at your feet – I pray that You'll continue to be with me and that You'll bring beauty from ashes, as my good friend, Mary, prayed for me at the very beginning of this ordeal.

Katie, Nickie and I made some Christmas candy today for several hours, and that was fun. Several times I thought of my dad, as he loved candy and the Christmas season, and I miss him, too, as he's been gone for almost 10 years. He would be so proud of his children and grandchildren.

This evening I helped with the high school Christmas party at church. Even though I really wasn't in the mood, I am so glad I went. It was fun and I enjoyed the company. Sometimes it is easy to just stay home by myself. That is probably a sign of some depression, but I know that is a natural emotion.

Lord, I know You have a plan for me and that it is better than anything I could ever imagine. I know that when I hurt, You hurt – in fact, I think I read that no tear I shed is in vain. I pray for Brady and his family. I know his parents are hurting, too. Help me to be content and joyful, even if You call me to a life of singleness. Help me to remember what Whitney told me, that maybe during this time, You have lessons to teach me. Maybe You want to show me my gifts and how You would have me use them. Maybe I need to be still and quiet and listen for Your voice. Please give me the strength and grace to get through this that only You can give me. Help me to really reflect You – for people to see You in me and be drawn to that.

December 11, 2005

I cried this morning . . . again. I couldn't even go to church! I was wallowing in my hurt and anger. So I stayed home and wrote to Whitney and then sat with a mug of hot chocolate and re-read Psalm 139. It was like reading it for the first time! I was reminded God made me with His hands and He knows me and He thinks about me and He has a plan for me! What an incredible reminder!

God, help me to never forget Your help and guidance and blessings and promises! Help me remember to thank You for all You have and will continue to do for me. Help me to truly know my gifts and how You want me to use them to glorify You, not me. Use me as an instrument to reflect You and Your goodness, mercy and love. I want to fall totally in love with you, Christ! Help me to do so and to radiate that! I don't want to miss out on Your plan, so help me focus and pay attention to what I need to do.

December 16, 2005

Debbie, my phone counselor, talked about God's mercy this week. She recalled how God revealed information about Brady to me the one week the men I work with were all gone on vacation (which has never happened in the history of the company), so I wouldn't cry or break down in front of them. God's mercy is truly amazing! Now, when I think of those words, "Wrapped up in your arms of grace" from a Chris Tomlin song,[9] what a picture – I feel God has me wrapped up in his love and protection!

Thank You, Lord, for these songs and how they minister to me and to so many others. Thank You for all the Christian artists. I pray they will know the impact their talents and willing hearts to glorify You are having on our world.

Debbie was correct. She said Brady would contact me before the holidays, and he did. He sent some photos back of the girls when they were younger and he addressed the note, "Dearest Annette" and then signed it, "With Love." I think he is delusional!

VI

A New Road

December 23, 2005 6:00 AM

I guess I am excited about Christmas, and that is why I am awake so early. Today I get to meet Whitney in person.

Thank You, Lord, for this new friendship. I can be so open and honest with her about my feelings. What a gift she has been to me. Thank You also for all of my friends. They have been so caring! What incredible blessings they each have been! Lord, You are so good to me. You love me and bless me and have forgiven me and want the best for me. You have not left me nor forsaken me and will not ever. Thank You! Lord, I want to delight in You. I want to do what You want me to do, whether that includes writing a book or teaching Bible studies, or singing more. Help me be so close to You that I will know where You are leading me and what You want me to do. Please help me to not be sad or over-emotional on Christmas or New Year's Eve. Help me to always remember Your love and be comforted by that. Thank you that you have brought total healing to Whitney and You allowed me to be a tiny part of that.

December 25, 2005 CHRISTMAS! 1:40 AM

Christmas Eve was a good day. I went to Christmas Eve service and it was wonderful, as always. It was so uplifting, and I truly left with a spirit of joy and thankfulness. Happy Birthday, Jesus!

January 2, 2006

Happy New Year! I am so ready! I spent New Year's Eve with dear friends and we had a great time. Thank you, Lord, for my friends. It was three couples and me, but they were great about not making me feel like the seventh wheel. I love them!

This morning I woke up thinking about the upcoming girls retreat and drafted an outline for a proposed schedule, and even wrote some notes in case I am asked to give a talk. I know the people planning this event may not want me to speak, as there may be someone more suitable, and that is fine. I may just send my outline to Steve (our Youth Minister) to get his feedback.

Lord, whatever You want me to do, help me be really OK with either decision and for my feelings to not get hurt if I am not needed at this event. Maybe You have someone else in mind for this. Lord, you know my heart, I just want each of the girls who attend to seriously look at themselves and see how they can come to know You more and to help them live lives you will be proud of and can use – I want them not to doubt Your unconditional love for them. That is my prayer for them, and if you can use me, help me to be aware of that.

Lord, use me and help me to know Your will, not mine. I fear I'll misinterpret what You want me to do. Help me to know if writing a book is from You. As you know, I have no idea how to go about writing a book, so if this is from You, please guide me every step. I won't be able to do it on my own. Like Chris Tomlin said in his book, "His agent is the Holy Spirit."[10] I'd like the same agent, please. I love you, Lord. Amen.

Thursday, January 12, 2006 10:15 PM

I'm feeling great! I am excited about this New Year and how God may use me. A group of us met at church to discuss the girls retreat. I was a little nervous because last week I had emailed Steve my proposed agenda and my offer to talk, as well as the notes I'd written. I was nervous because I had not heard back from him and I didn't know what he or the other ladies would think about it.

When the meeting started, he said the lady they asked to speak was still unsure. I didn't know if that meant he did not receive my email or he didn't like the idea of me speaking, so my heart sort of fell. But later as we went through the plans, he'd printed off my proposed schedule with some adjustments and mentioned how I'd emailed him a draft "talk." He read it and thought it was really good and said he'd been wanting me to do something but wanted me to be sure I was ready. He said I was respected, well-known, and loved at Fern Creek Christian, so he'd love for me to do the talk. I am excited but nervous. I'll be praying God will use me to speak His truths and message to those girls. And, I know I can do anything through Christ who gives me strength! Maybe I'll do really well and will get to speak more. Maybe this is a new talent God has given me.

I will definitely be stepping out of my comfort zone. I can't help but think that since I woke up and immediately wrote the talk on New Year's Day that God gave me the words.

On a more personal note, Lord, help me to be so in love with You that not having a man in my life is OK. Help me to know Your plan for my life and give me wisdom and discernment and patience, too. Amen.

Sunday, January 15, 2006   10:15 PM

Lord, I am already nervous about my "talk" at the girls retreat in February. I want to do a good job – of course getting praise from my friends would be great, but Lord, I really want to communicate to them Your faithfulness, Your love and whatever they need to hear. Please guide me as I tweak my talk. I want to speak whatever it is You want me to say. I pray for each girl who will attend – that they will hear whatever message You have for them. Please be glorified through me – not just with my talk, but every day, help me to exude Your grace, goodness, faithfulness, patience, kindness, mercy, understanding and forgiveness. I truly desire for people to see You when they look into my eyes.

Today's sermon spoke so directly to me! Rick Burdett, my minister, mentioned Paul was not an eloquent speaker but he was eager to preach the gospel because of his testimony – because of what Christ had done in his life. The power of God saves, not the messenger. So, help me to be bolder and more confident. (Talk about timing!)

Thursday, January 19, 2006

Tonight I had dinner with Angela and Chase, my accountant friends. We had so much fun. I met both of these ladies through my job. I met Angela about eight years ago and Chase about two years ago. They are both amazing Christian women and I am so thankful that the Lord brought them into my life (and He used accounting, so He definitely has a sense of humor!)

One day about three years ago, Angela was showing me the house she had purchased and all of a sudden started asking about Southeast Christian Church. I am not comfortable with "evangelizing" as I don't know all the answers, but I was honest and told her how God has blessed me and about what a wonderful place it is. She was interested in going, but it is a huge church and she was sort of frightened to go by herself (understandably). I offered to go with her and have breakfast after the service. So one cool October Sunday morning, we went; and in a couple of months, she was baptized. Praise God! And she has thrown herself into it like no one I've ever seen. She immediately volunteered in the children's ministry and went on a two-week mission trip to Poland that summer.

My point here is that the only reason I think she asked me about church was because during the years we'd worked together, my faith was a very evident part of my life. For example, she knew I went on a mission trip to Mexico during spring break with the youth group, and she'd heard me talk about Bible studies I'd enjoyed. She was also working with many other Christian people (such as Chase) and she has a respect for them and their work. Which brings me to another point I heard a young minister say years ago.

If people don't respect our work, they won't respect our God. So to be a witness for Christ, we don't have to always be "preaching" at people, we need to be actually living what we believe.

At dinner, Angela told me the coolest thing. She actually wrote a letter to Bob Russell, the long-time pastor at Southeast Christian Church (who baptized me almost 19 years ago, and is one of my heroes) and explained how she came to SECC in part because of me! Wow! Thank You, Lord, for her telling me this. She then explained he read a portion of her letter as part of his sermon one Sunday. Amazing! What an honor! She has grown in her relationship with God and is leaving in a few weeks for Japan where she feels she is being led to teach English.

Lord, please be with her the entire way. Please give her a peace from You, and I pray she will never doubt Your presence. Help this to be the experience of a lifetime for her. Thank You for the incredible privilege of being in her life.

She told me she thinks God has a wonderful plan for me. Lord, I agree with her, so please help me not to miss it. Chase said that maybe I will get to speak and be Louisville's "Beth Moore." Wow – to even be mentioned in the same sentence with this amazing woman of God is a huge honor. From the first time I heard her speak several years ago, I thought, "I want a faith and a love relationship with Christ like she has." I love this idea except the idea of speaking in public scares me to death. The wild thing is, several other people lately have mentioned this same thing. Then they said, "You could really speak to women who have been in your situation . . . maybe you should write a book." Hello, there is that whole book idea again.

I've thought about this and will pray that You will guide me and if this is Your plan, help me to know without a shadow of a doubt. But, Lord, I don't want to think more highly of myself than I ought to, so help me to always remain grounded and humbled by You and Your grace, goodness, love and mercy.

Another friend also wrote, "I do think you should think of the book idea. And then you could hit the speaking circuit. I have often thought about what a witness you have been to me and could be to all women who are tempted by the devil to think, 'nope, not telling my story . . . no one wants to hear from a divorcee'. I find myself in social situations thinking 'how do I skirt the issue of a previous marriage?' God can really use you to help women realize that God is there for them when a husband isn't, and to forgive themselves, forgive the situation and move onward and upward."

In my opinion, divorce is a private matter, so I don't think you owe it to the world to tell about it. It is perfectly fine just to say, "I am single." Obviously you will have to tell some people eventually, but when you are meeting people for the first time, you have every right to keep that part of your life to yourself. I told a friend this, and I think it gave her some relief. She has been remarried to a wonderful man for several years now. That part of her life is over. God has healed her and wants her to move "onward and upward" and enjoy the abundant life He has given her.

Sunday, January 22, 2006   10:00 PM

Tonight's small group study was about being in a cave – a dark, lonely place of shelter – and that God is with us when we are there. I finally opened up and told the group

I'd been in the cave for about a year, and although it has been the toughest year of my life, God has truly been right with me and has been so evident. It was a great study!

February 6, 2006

I read the coolest quote from the book *Falling In Love with Jesus.*[11] It said, "God does not usually instantly pull us out of the 'wilderness', as while we are there is when our faith truly grows." I concur.

Wednesday, February 8, 2006 10:35 PM

Today Whitney reminded me in an email that God may want me all to Himself for a while to nourish me, and He is getting me ready for the rest of my life and all He has in store for me. She added He is probably like a parent at Christmas when we can't wait for our children to open and delight in a gift we have for them . . .He is anticipating my reaction . . . one of thankfulness. Wow! To think that God, the Creator of all, would feel that way about me is amazing! The part about wanting me all to Himself right now goes along with the book I'm reading called, *Falling in Love With Jesus.* It is incredible.

Lord, You know my heart and my desire is to know You more and to be more like You. I want to exude You. I want people to see me but to really see You and Your grace, patience, forgiveness, sincerity, love, concern, joy.

Lord, please be with the girls retreat. Please have Your hand on every detail. Help us adult sponsors to exude You. Please speak to the girls through us, and the speakers. Please be with me and help me to not be too nervous. I know I can do anything through Christ who gives me strength. I believe this talk is from You, so help me to do my best for You. Help it to not glorify me, but to show Your goodness, love and kindness. I love You, Lord. Amen.

I feel so great about my life – I don't ever remember feeling as confident (but not cocky) or joy-filled. God is awesome – He is so concerned about each of his children that He gives us His peace!

Thursday, February 9, 2006 10:15 p.m.

Tonight I have been reading *Falling In Love With Jesus.* In Chapter 8, Kathy Troccoli describes her encounter with Mother Theresa and how beautiful she was because she had invited Jesus to radiate through her – He is her beauty. Wow! My prayer lately is I want to exude Christ – when people see me or meet me they would see Christ in me – through my eyes – they'd see His love, patience, joy, mercy and peace.

Lord, You are so amazing to me – like You are only focusing on me! Wow! Thank You. Please don't stop – please continue to look down on me with love, and I hope You enjoy my response of awe! Oh how I hope I never lose that response to You and Your provision, goodness, peace, love and forgiveness! Please continue to draw me closer to You so I won't miss out on anything You want me to learn or do during this time of wilderness. Lord, You know my heart. You know I want this girls retreat to be great – that each girl who attends will hear the message you have for them. Please be with me and help me not to be nervous and to do a great job with my talk for Your glory. Help Nickie not to be embarrassed by me or what I say. Am I making too much of a big deal out of this? I just know these 30 or so girls are important to You; they are Your children. So I truly hope we can reach them with Your truths. Guide all of the women helping at the retreat to be models of You.

Lord, You are a huge God and I praise You and thank You for all You've done for me and for all You have planned for me. Truly help me to be content and joy-filled no matter what Your plan is for me, please. My big prayers are: 1) if You want me to write a book that You'll orchestrate it, 2) that if You want me to be a speaker, that You'd handle all those details.

Please be with Angela as she travels to Japan today. Keep her safe and her eyes on You. Thank You for her boldness and commitment to You!

On the drive to work today, I couldn't help but notice the beautiful sunrise. I'm trying to notice them more often. The colors were so pretty and a light was shining down from the heavens onto the earth – it was truly gorgeous. I wondered to myself, "How many people even notice this? I wonder if God just creates these beautiful scenes in the sky and wonders when we'll notice them . . . and Him?"

Monday, February 13, 2006

A year ago today is the last time I hugged and kissed Brady. I remember we had just sat through a worship service at Southeast Christian. The topic was "Integrity in Marriage." Numerous couples who had been married to each other for 20+ years were on the platform being honored (and rightfully so). It was a beautiful service, and I cried all the way through it, thinking we'd work things out and some day maybe we could be one of those couples. It was a service that gave me hope, but I believe Brady was feeling a different emotion. I believe God used this beautiful service about His design for marriage to convict him that he could not "string me along" anymore. After church, we went to lunch together at Don Pablos (which soon thereafter closed, and I just think that is interesting) then we visited his parents and went back to the church so he could get his truck. He gave me a box of Godiva chocolates and a Valentine card that said, "I'm glad we're in this together." He had signed it, "I love you." Later that night he called me. We talked for a few moments, but there were no more phone conversations after that. He had his cell phone disconnected the very next day.

It doesn't seem like it has been a year ago, since the details are so vivid in my mind. I even remember what he was wearing. I remember crying when he arrived at church, and I remember tears streaming down my face during the service. This year my Valentine will be Jesus. I am His and He is mine. And knowing the Lord wants me as His is an amazing thought in itself!

Lord, I truly want to get to know You more. Please rule my life and show me Your ways, Your truths, Your lessons and Your plan for my life. Help me to remain excited about learning more about You. I truly do not want to worship the idea of having a mate, so keep me from that – help me to always only worship You, the Creator, my Savior. But I hope it is OK to admire men with a heart sold out to You.

Please be with all those who do not have a significant other, especially tomorrow – Valentine's Day (also un-affectionately referred to by me as Singles Awareness Day) and help them remember and feel Your most incredible and complete, love. Amen.

I received the following acrostic via email:

"For God so loV ed the world,
That He gA ve
His On Ly
BegottE n
SoN
That whosever
Believeth I n Him
Should N ot perish,
But have E verlasting life." John 3:16

Tuesday, February 15, 2006

This morning I woke up and was praying to my huge God about my big dreams. Then on the way to work, I was listening to one of the Passion CDs and was singing along to Chris Tomlin's "God is Bigger Than"[12] song and it suddenly hit me what I was actually singing about – the hugeness of God. He is "bigger than the air I breathe, the world I'll leave." I've been singing along to this song for a couple of months, but the implication of the words just hit me.

At work, I received an email from Southeast Christian Church called "Your Work Journey". This weekend I'll give my talk at the girls retreat entitled, "**God Is In Control**," so this email was very timely. Here are a couple of lines from the email. "*Did you know your life is under divine necessity?* ***God is in control.*** *The difference between Jesus and the rest of us is that Jesus always followed God's path. We have a habit of trying to lead our own lives. But God is gracious. He keeps bringing us back to the path marked, 'Follow'. Take a moment to review your own journey.* ***Can you see God's hand directing events in your life? Were there times when your path was altered unexpectedly but now you see God was pushing you to follow?*** *Now look ahead. Do you know where you are going? Are you following God's footsteps on your journey?* ***Do you have a sense of what you must do?***"

How amazing that the God of the universe cares so much about me He orchestrates these little details to confirm a plan for me. You, Lord, are truly awesome!

Sunday, February 19, 2006   10:15 p.m.

I can't believe it has been almost a week since I have journaled. It has, however, been a busy week getting ready for the girls retreat. It went really well and I praise You, Lord, and thank You as Your hand was all over it. None of us had ever planned such an event before, so its' success was all You.

My talk did not go how I had planned it in my mind. I thought I would be behind a podium and could walk around and that I'd be a strong presenter of the message. But, about 45 minutes before I was to speak, I got emotional. I told Nickie I wanted her to read it to be sure it did not embarrass her. She was not embarrassed at all. So we did some worship time, and I felt a calming in my spirit. When it was time for me to speak, I walked to the front of the room and bowed my head and asked them to join me in prayer. Tears came to my eyes and I had to wait until I could compose myself to speak. After my teary prayer, I was able to speak and I think conveyed most of my talk as I had written it. I was disappointed in myself and felt I had failed for getting emotional and hoped I hadn't embarrassed Nickie, but everyone said I did a great job. Gina even said I was a great communicator. So, maybe me being so human and vulnerable was better – when I am weak, God is strong! Maybe He used this broken vessel to touch someone who needed to see this broken woman truly loves God and knows no matter what the past held for her, she knows without a doubt God is still in control.

I love You, Lord, and praise You and thank You for all You've done for me and for all You still have ahead for me. Holy Spirit, please be with me each day and mold me into a woman after God's own heart.

Also, I'm praying in Your perfect time, you'll reveal a book title to me. You know my desire is to help others who have and will walk in my shoes. I long to bring them hope and faith in You as You have been so evident to me. Amen.

Monday, February 20, 2006 11:00 AM

God, Help me to be calm and content and to love the time You want me all to yourself to behold You – so I can truly become like You. You are amazing – You are huge, Creator, and yet You orchestrate every little detail in my life. Help me to always give You the glory. Amen.

Tuesday, February 21, 2006 10:40 PM

Today I received a cool email from SECC called, "Planning For Success at Work" but it really isn't about work for me. It's more about planning for successfully knowing God's will for me. The email explains we might have a great idea, even a worthy one, but if it is not God's plan for us it will fail. Jesus came to do the will of the Father only and that needs to be my goal – to truly seek God's will for me – then it will surely succeed! So, I need to stay in His word, stay connected to Him, and to discover His mind on the matter. Also, I need to get the plan confirmed by others! Wow – so many people have told me to write a book.

(OK, so this is wild. As I'm typing this, a man called into a local radio station and just asked the host how to know God's will for his life. She responded it would not go against scripture, to find out what his passions are, have it confirmed by others, and watch for open and closed doors. Lord, are you now using the radio to speak to me?)

Several people have mentioned the speaking idea, too (including Chase and Angela), and LuAnn mentioned last night she thinks I'll do more of that.

Lord, You know my heart is to do Your will with my life. So if I am to speak/write a book, so be it. I am Yours to mold and use as You see fit. These things seem like extraordinary undertakings for a no name like me, but if it is Your will, I have faith You will see them through. Help me to see Your vision and each step as You light one at a time as a lamp unto my path. But if these are not Your plans or maybe they are on a smaller scale, help me to truly never think more highly of myself than I ought and to be satisfied and content with that too if that is Your plan for me. In fact, there sometimes is no more of an ordinary feeling or job than raising our children day in and day out, but what an extraordinary job and blessing to help mold another human – to teach them about You so that they someday can share Your love and message with people they will meet. I love You, Lord. Please keep me focused on You and to truly seek and find Your will for me. Amen.

Friday, February 24, 2006

Tonight I read quite a bit from the book, *Forever in Love With Jesus,* and it was amazing. The thought that spoke most to me tonight was, "give your time and attention to what God is doing right now and don't get worked up about what may or may not happen tomorrow." [13] For me this isn't about worrying, but it is more about thinking ahead to the future and His plan for the rest of my life (writing a book, speaking to women). In Chris Tomlin's book, *The Way I Was Made*, he said trying to be in control of our future is something we need to confess as sin.[14] So, what does God want me doing right now? Maybe I need to start typing my notes (which I have) and then if He leads me and puts it all together as a book to encourage and bring Him glory, that would be great. I'd love to be used by Him in that way. What an honor and privilege that would be.

I am reading and learning a lot more about Him, so I'm sure that is pleasing to Him. In fact, tonight I read Psalm 19:14, "*May the words of my mouth and the meditation of my heart be pleasing in Your sight, O Lord . . .*" This is my prayer – that I am pleasing Him each day by reading good books and from the Bible but also by performing the "ordinary" tasks of life such as working, raising children, cleaning, cooking and being a good employee and friend.

This brings me to the book's point that hit me the hardest. Kathy Troccoli says not to focus on "quiet time" when we read the daily scripture but to instead "practice His presence." Wow! I love this and want to do this. It makes me think of the theme of John 15:1-8 where Jesus tells us He is the vine and we are the branches, and our job is to "remain in Him" for without being connected to Him (our life source) we will die and bear no fruit. He even says that without Him, we can do nothing.

I heard a preacher on the radio (Kyle Idleman from Southeast Christian Church) say we are simply to "abide". No matter what, we are to abide. He explained this sounds so simple, but it is so hard. We get impatient and want to *do* something, but sometimes we are simply to stay connected to Jesus, to trust Him and allow His power to work through us. And when we have done this, there is the coolest promise! Verse 7 says, "*But if you remain in me and my words remain in you, you may ask for anything you want and it will be granted!*" There is a catch here. I think when someone initially reads this, they think, great! I want a new car and a bigger house and a raise.

But I believe if we have really spent time in God's presence, these material things become trivial and instead of those, our heart desires to be more like God. We ask for things like the ability to love as He loves or to forgive as He does. We desire the things that He desires for us. Amazing.

Lord, You know my heart and You know it desires to be more like You. I want to exude You and Your wonderful characteristics to others. Please light my path You have for me and help me to be focused on You. Again, help me not to miss anything You want me to learn or do. I feel close to You and I look forward to my journaling and quiet time and although I can't always be on a mountaintop experience, I don't want to ever lose this closeness and desire to search Your word to know what You want from me. My life is Yours to mold into a beautiful "masterpiece." What a great word and thought. Thank You for the many blessings You have given me. I love you. Amen.

Sunday, February 26, 2006 7:50 PM

I received an email from Whitney on how she went to the Women Of Faith conference this weekend and really enjoyed it. She said Tammy Trent told her story of losing her husband in a tragic accident and how she had healed from that. Whitney said she kept thinking of me – no one touched on divorce and the pain and rejection that comes with it, so she can see me doing this someday. Lord, is it OK for me to think about this? I really never want to think more highly of myself than I ought as I know that I am a sinner and I deserve death, but only because of Your amazing unfailing love for me, I have the promise of eternal life in heaven with You!

Lord, I want to be used by You however You want – if it is on a smaller scale teaching Juniors and Seniors Sunday School, help me to do my best to reach them, to love them and accept them. Maybe eventually You'll want me to lead a Bible study. (Note: in 2008 I was asked to facilitate a women's Bible study.) *Lord, it occurred to me that in October of 2004, I sang, "Here I Am" for special music and now this is truly my prayer – Here I am, use me!*

This week I want to start typing up my journal to see if You will make a book out of it, Lord, and I pray You will tell me exactly what to write, and what to edit out. Keep me focused on bringing hope and encouragement by showing Your touches and control of my life and my complete surrender to You. Help me to be real and to bring glory and honor to Your name. My story is Yours, so please tell me what You want told. If there are things I have forgotten but You want them in, please bring them to my mind. Help me to know Your will and feel Your peace. Amen.

VII

New Blessings!

Tuesday, February 28, 2006 6:30 p.m.

Gina left today for Mexico for two months, Katie is at school in Cincinnati, and Nickie will be at Southeast Christian from 6 – 10 pm nearly every night from tonight through the length of the Easter pageant. So for the next month I'll be alone . . . a lot. Maybe this is the time for me to start typing my notes. Why am I so nervous about starting this? Am I afraid to fail? There really is no failing with this – if it doesn't become a book, maybe it will just be therapeutic for me to type them up. Maybe I'm a little nervous there isn't a big plan for me – maybe I just get to be ordinary – but that is really OK, too. I've probably just daydreamed too much! Maybe my journal will just be used to help one other woman, and that would be so worth it.

Last night we watched the final episode of *The Bachelor* and out of nowhere my feelings of rejection and hurt came up as I watched Mona sob when she did not get chosen by Travis, the handsome bachelor doctor. She was devastated and said how it hurts to trust someone, to open up and then get crushed. When I went to bed I cried. How many other people have felt this rejection? As I lay there trying to go to sleep, God gave me an image. The bachelor gave Sarah a diamond ring on a necklace, as he was not ready to make a promise (of marriage and forever) that he didn't know yet if he could keep. I admired his honesty and sincerity and the sacredness in which he viewed the marriage covenant, but God, our bridegroom, can and does make a promise He will keep. He wants to spend forever with us, and when we accept Him, He washes us clean and snow-white (liked a wedding dress). I wonder if He will hug us and twirl us around when we get to heaven because He will be so happy to be with us. What a vision!

I know if I were married or dating right now, a lot of this time I get to spend with God, I would most likely be spending with either my husband or boyfriend. So this single time is a blessing for me. I really can't give myself to someone when I have so much to work on and to learn. I think Whitney was right when she said, "maybe God wants you all to Himself right now." Maybe it is so I can write a book, maybe it is just so I can learn more truths about Him and learn to love Him as deeply as possible and to totally depend on Him and not any man. Maybe it is to mold me into being totally content right where I am. Maybe it is so He can also mold my future mate into the person He wants him to be, a man after God's own heart. That's the kind of man I want someday to spend the rest of my life with, if that is God's plan for me. I will have incredibly high standards before I even start to date again, if I ever date again. Lord, I'll leave this in Your hands and pray for Your wisdom when and if that time comes.

Friday, March 3, 2006

Today I was in a good mood all day. Yesterday was the same, and I was so excited about Nickie's scholarship news (she received a partial scholarship to Georgetown College) and it was fun to share that. However on Wednesday I was a little down (before Nickie's news) and I really don't know why. I need to remember that every day can't be a mountaintop experience – there will be some sad or down days, and that is just a part of life here on earth.

Saturday, March 4, 2006 11:35 am

I just returned home from walking with LuAnn at the gym. We walked 3 miles. I'm not sure we're up to the running, but we can at least walk and talk for 3 miles! (I'm sure the talking part doesn't surprise anyone!)

Today I'm thinking about that un-noticed life and humility. *Lord, You know I've been praying for Your will but also that if You want me to write a book, I'll do it. If you want me to speak, I'll do it. If you want to give me a song that praises You, I'll do it – but in all these things You'd have to work in and through me as I don't know how to do any of these on my own. I can see myself with a book and it being a success in helping and encouraging others going through separation and divorce, and I can see me speaking someday (only through Your power and strength) and using these painful divorce experiences to help other women. But Lord, maybe I have the wrong vision – maybe I'll write or speak to small audiences and live an "un-noticed" life. If this is your plan, help me to be totally OK with that,* *and thankful if I am able to help only one person! I never want to become prideful.* ***see Dec 30, 2006!**

Please reign in my life, Lord. Help me to be humble; never let me forget I am a sinner and You, precious Savior, loved me so much You took my sin on Your back and You died my death. Help me to be more like You and to serve You all the days of my life. Amen

Sunday, March 5, 2006

Today in church we studied Romans 8:28-39. What an amazing section of scripture! One verse that particularly stands out in my mind is verse 32: "*He did not spare his own Son, but gave Him up for us – how will He not also along with Him, graciously give us all things.*" I like to put that together with Psalms 25:12:14: "*Who then is the man that fears the Lord? He will instruct him in the ways chosen for him. He will spend his days in prosperity, and his descendants will inherit the land. The Lord confides in those who fear him; he makes his covenant known to them.*" I fear the Lord and desire to do His will and claim Him as my Savior, so I believe He wants to give me the desires of my heart.

Monday, March 06, 2006

Today I noticed I had missed a call from Brady yesterday, as I had left my cell phone in my car (thankfully). I told Stan, one of my bosses, that I'll probably receive an email from him today. I figured it would be about taxes, but hey, he is a big boy so he can just figure it out on his own. At 11:55 a.m. I received the expected email.

The timing was perfect because at noon I was already scheduled to call my phone counselor, Debbie. She said she feels like he has just been dumped and is looking to see if there is a crack in the door where he can get back in. She said when a "new door" closes, often times the spouse who left the marriage tries going back to the "old door." She also said this tells her he isn't done. He'll probably still contact me.

We also talked about my feelings after watching "The Bachelor," when Mona was rejected and hurting. She said it is normal for those feelings to come back up. She said we fear being rejected even as a child, so when we actually face it, it is very painful.

I told her about Nickie's scholarships and she, too, was amazed. I told her I've always wanted to be able to pay for my girls' college, but never dreamed I'd actually be able to. It looks like at least for the first year, I'll be able to do this and not have to get a student loan. I've told several people this reminds me of Psalms 25, "*When we delight ourselves in the Lord, he gives us the desires of our heart.*" She said, "God, your husband, has stepped in and provided." He has in so many ways.

Wednesday, March 8, 2006

Today my van died! I had it towed to the mechanic to be fixed. I have had to add gallons of coolant to it the last several days but there is no dripping on my garage floor, so I thought, "wonder where all this coolant is going?" This afternoon the mechanic called and told me he had found the answer. It was draining into the motor and mixing with the oil. Now I'm no Einstein when it comes to anything about automobiles, but I knew that did not sound good. The mechanic confirmed my fears and said that I need a new engine! What?! He had kindly researched this for me and found a used one at a junk- yard, but it would still cost around $3,000! So, I told him to let me think about it. This news immediately brought tears to my eyes so I called my brother, Jimmy, for help. He calmly told me my van was only worth about $500, so it would not be a wise move for me to repair it. I asked Dave, the mechanic, to just put some oil in it and some coolant so I can drive if for a few days, as this would leave me car-less. He kindly laughed (and probably thought I was an idiot and clueless about cars) and said, "You can't drive the van – the engine could blow up." Oh, that got my attention. So I hung up and cried. You see, I've had my van for years. It was like a part of me. I've put over 100,000 miles on it and, most of those miles were toting my girls and their friends to church and to youth camps and to the Billy Graham Crusade, etc. I have some great memories in that van. It was like an old, comfortable pair of ratty jeans. So I grieved . . . but not for long. . .

My daughter, Nickie, came to pick me up from work in her car and saw I was sad, so she drove me to a dealership where there were a couple of cute sports cars I mentioned I'd like to look at when it was time for me to car shop. I knew my van was getting old, and, frankly, I've had "new/used" car fever for several months. However, I wanted to be smart, do my research, and take my time. We looked at the sports cars and they were really nice, but a little pricy for me. As we turned to leave, though, (imagine dramatic music here and us turning to leave in slow motion like in a love story) there it was in all its radiant glory . . . my dream car! It was a beauty. It was a two-year-old Mazda RX8 and in immaculate shape. Apparently a young man had just traded it in for a car with more horsepower (whatever that is). I tried to maintain a serious composure (you don't want to seem too eager and tipoff the salesperson), but as soon as he unlocked it and I sat in it, I was beaming! I told him I'd think about it, and I tried to sound like I knew what I was talking about as I asked about the rotary engine and the life of such low-profile tires. We left and I went from tears to not being able to wipe the smile off my silly face in just a matter of a few hours. I was reminded of that scripture, "Weeping lasts for a night, but joy comes in the morning," except my weeping only lasted for about two hours! Yes!

In the meantime, God is still providing for me. My boss' son has a spare car he is getting ready to sell, so he has offered to let me use it for a few weeks until I can get the vehicle of my dreams.

Sunday, March 12, 2006

Today's sermon was on Romans 12:1-8 and was entitled, "Crawling Off The Altar". It was great. Rick used two scriptures I have thought of often this past year and have included in my journaling the last couple of months. They are Romans 12:2: "*Do not conform to the pattern of this world but be transformed by the renewing of your mind,*" and 12:3: "*. . . Do not think of yourself more highly than you ought . . .*" The first verse I haven't written about specifically, but I have been thinking about what I am putting into my mind. I am mainly listening to Christian music, I am reading Christian books, and I am spending quiet time at night reading the Bible. I have an inner joy, and it makes so much sense that if I am feeding my mind Godly material, I will only be able to speak of those things. "*From the overflow of the heart, the mouth speaks.*" (Matthew 12:34) I totally want to exude Christ in my life.

The second verse I have thought about as I've learned to begin to pray big prayers because I have a big God. I've prayed about writing a book, speaking to women and marrying again some day. I realize I don't deserve any of these things and that is where I need to remain humbled at who I am, a sinner who only by the blood of Christ, has the promise of eternal life.

My minister, Rick, explained in his sermon that to be a living sacrifice comes from an attitude of gratitude. When I remember the mercy of God that has been poured into my life, it brings joy, making me want to live a life of worship for Him . . . to give Him my all! He talked about knowing God's will for our lives and that in order for us know this we have to have faith. God promises wisdom if we ask Him for it. He talked about us being members of the body of Christ and we each have special God-given gifts. He suggested we each need to discover what our spiritual gift is . . . what are our passions? He suggested asking our friends this question to help us discover our gifts.

He also told us not to forget any tough experiences we have been through, that instead of forgetting them, help others going through the same thing. It is called ministry. He explained that only when we find out what our gifts are and use them for God, will we discover our purpose and be complete. "I become what I worship," says Louie Gigleo in his book, *The Air I Breathe.*[15]

Tuesday, March 14, 2006

Yesterday, while at the gym, I asked LuAnn what she thought my spiritual gift is (after Rick suggested this in his sermon Sunday) and she said, "speaking." She said she would have never said this until after she heard me speak at the girls retreat. She said there are so many women out there who are hurting as wives, mothers, or all alone.

Lord, do You want me to be used somehow for this? If so, please give me Your vision and all it would take to do Your will in bringing Your message of hope, peace, truth, comfort and love to these precious daughters of Yours. I am Yours. I know if a plan is not from You, it will fail, so I pray for Your wisdom.

Thursday, March 16, 2006

Today I got my new/used car! Lord, again thank You for your provision and gifts. I was able to pay cash for it, and it is my dream car! Lord, You just continue to pour out blessings on me and I am so grateful, but I know I am so undeserving. Help me to always give You praise for your goodness in my life. I was going to have my brothers go with me to negotiate the price, but they had other plans and could go another time. But then I thought to myself, "I can do this. I am a grown independent woman, for heaven's sake. I can negotiate a car purchase." And so I did, and I got it for $500 under my budget! You see, I wasn't really alone . . . God was right there with me, just like He is every moment of every day.

Friday, March 17, 2006 11:15 P.M.

I'm waiting for Nickie to come home from opening night at the Southeast Easter Pageant. I have been by myself since I left work at 3 p.m. today, and I've really enjoyed it. I've typed some of my journaling notes into the computer in case God makes a book out of them. Then, I pick up

Chris Tomlin's book[16] and opened to page 143. It says, "Sometimes God will use your strengths. Sometimes He'll use your weaknesses. But either way, there are things that you can say and people you can say them to that no one else can. . . and whatever you have to give is God's very best gift for others – probably many others in this world."[17] Wow! I can't help but think of how I could use my life experiences to encourage other single moms and divorced women.

I've been wondering a lot lately what my future holds. On the same page he says, "I was not made to know my future or to control it . . . Even on days we can't see it, God is at his work in our lives . . . He knows our heart's deepest desires. He sees what you and I could never see . . . God will move mountains to put you where He wants you. If God has something that He wants you to do, He'll give you a platform to do it."[17] A "platform" . . . this sounds like maybe a book and/or speaking for me possibly.

This message just feels like it is for me, Lord. You know my heart's desire is to encourage others and to proclaim how You have blessed me and how You want to do the same for them if they'll put their trust in You. Help me to be patient and to know Your perfect timing and what to do in the meantime. I don't want to run ahead of You, and I don't want to miss what You want me to do.

Saturday, March 18, 2006 11:40 p.m.

Today Nickie and I drove the new car to Lexington to shop, and we had a great time. I am treasuring times like these with her since she will graduate from high school in a couple of months, and then soon will be off to college. I can't imagine her not being here. We are so close and she is such an incredible blessing to me.

Lord, thank you for her and for her deep faith and convictions to live in a way that is pleasing to You. Please continue to grow her faith in You.

Monday, March 20, 2006

Today I went for my annual "female doctor's appointment." It has been almost two years since I'd been. I was surprised at the emotions that came up when I told the nurse and my doctor that my husband had left me and how he may have been cheating, so I needed to be tested in case he gave me some sort of disease. I cried! The pain of being rejected and the shame of having to admit my husband left me was so great! I could hardly talk. My doctor was very kind and patient with me until I was finally able to gain my composure and get the words out. The nurse was an older lady and after I told her, I apologized for my tears and she smiled at me and patted my arm and said, "Oh honey, you didn't do anything wrong . . . some men are just pigs!" I liked her immediately. My doctor doesn't think I have contracted any disease because he said I most likely would have already seen some symptoms, so that is a praise!

I emailed one of my best friends about these emotions and told her I guess this is one of the situations Christ was talking about when He said we are to forgive seventy times seven times. The actual sin against us has already taken place, but then a situation comes along that reminds us of the pain we originally felt. So, I know I need to pray for Brady and also for the Holy Spirit to help me to again forgive him for hurting me. I think I'll do this tomorrow. Today I want to punch him or at least find a punching bag with his picture on it and punch the day lights out of it! My wise friend told me she thinks Satan uses these feelings of shame and rejection to get in the way of forgiveness. She is so correct. This shame rears its ugly head so often for me. I never want anyone to think I am a bad person or wonder what I did that would cause my husband to leave me. And what about the future? What if God has a man for me and I have to explain it to him? What will his initial thoughts of me be? I just have to trust if God has a godly man for me, he will come to know me and love me for the person I am and realize that I didn't do anything to deserve such treatment. I'm not for one second suggesting that I am perfect, but I know in my heart I was the best wife I knew how to be.

It hurts to the core to truly realize the person I committed myself to, the one I totally trusted with my heart and life, the person who I was going to spend the rest of my life with, the person who I couldn't wait to share good news with, the person I thought I knew so well, the person I couldn't wait to get to hold his hand while I fell to sleep at night, did not share my commitment or value me enough to treat me with the respect a husband is supposed to have for his wife. In fact he treated me with no respect at all. I have learned he has told hurtful lies about me to his coworkers. It still hurts to know the last couple of years of our marriage, of my life, were a lie. But Lord, You were betrayed by one of your closest friends, a disciple, Judas Iscariot, so you know how I feel. You have been in these shoes; You know the pain first hand. And yet You chose to forgive him and us as we betray you daily. Truly amazing!

Tonight as I was making homemade spaghetti and meatballs (just the meatballs are home-made so don't be overly impressed) I got a surprise call from Tina, my first counselor. It was so great to hear from her. I had written her a letter (yes, an actual letter) and she had just received it and was calling to check in. One of the first things she said was, "I hope you write that book!" Funny! I told her I'm working on putting my notes in the computer to see if God makes a book from it. She was so encouraging and wants to have lunch with me soon. She told me that she just loved me. How cool to hear this from a counselor!

Lord, my prayer is I will consider You the love of my life. Only You will not ever disappoint me or leave me or hurt me. In fact, you have a plan to give me life abundantly. Praise You for Your unfailing love for me and for all of Your children. Thank you for being right with me and for carrying me this last year. Your blessings have been unbelievable, and I am so thankful for the mercy and grace and kindness You continue to show me. I realize I am so unworthy. However, if You have a man for me, help me to be ready and to have wisdom to know that He is from You. I love you and praise You, my Big Huge God! Amen.

Friday, March 24, 2006 9:55 p.m.

Today I had some oral surgery done. It wasn't bad. Of course I'm still on pain medication, so I may be feeling bad tomorrow. I am a wimp when it comes to any type of surgery and pain . . . and needles! But this morning I just told myself if Christ could be whipped and beaten like He was, I can certainly endure a little dental pain. But my dentist was good – I barely felt the needle at all.

Last night I was reading the book called, *The Air I Breathe* by Louie Giglio.[18] It is very good and talks about how all of us are worshipers; that we were made that way, so we each worship something or someone. Interesting.

Lord, my desire is to worship You, The Creator, and I long to be like You. Like when the silversmith purifies the metal so that he can see his face in it, I want to be so much like You, so clean and pure, that people can see You when they look at me. Maybe that is one reason You have brought me through this "fire." You in Your wisdom know that in order to draw extremely close to you, we have to go through trials we cannot handle on our own. Thank You for loving me enough to be right with me through it all! I am humbled at Your goodness and love and provisions for me.

Wednesday, March 29, 2006 8:19 p.m.

I spoke with Debbie, my phone counselor, on Monday, and she can't believe how God continues to provide for me. In fact, she said He has blessed me with unusual prosperity! She was impressed I went to the car dealership by myself and negotiated a price (and got it for $500 under my budget, mind you). I was able to get Katie situated in her apartment and school in Cincinnati, and I've got Nickie's college plans in the works. She said not many women would be able to do any of these things by themselves. Wow, I'd never thought of that. I told her since I was a single mom at the young age of 25, with two little girls depending on me, I never thought giving up was an option – I had to go on, including working two jobs at one point, to provide for them. I also said maybe that was a downfall of mine in my marriage – I was too independent. Not that I'm saying the way I was treated by my husband is justified, but maybe if God has a future relationship for me, I need to remember to not be too independent, but I don't want to become dependent either. Maybe I could just be interdependent.

Debbie reminded me that my future is bright. And this reminded me of Job 42:12, "*. . . and the Lord blessed his later years more than the first.*" Wow – now that is a promise I'm claiming! I am excited about my future. I mean I am only 40 (OK I'll be 41 in 3 days, but who's counting) and my daughters are almost all grown and out of the house, so I can't imagine what all God has in store for me. I remember clearly how one day last summer my boss said to me, "God has big plans for you." That has just stuck in my mind. It goes right along with the Bible study I attended this winter where I learned that if I believe in a big God, then I won't be afraid to pray big prayers. I've been doing that ever since.

I also told Debbie about how painful it was to admit to my gynecologist I needed tests to be sure I hadn't been infected with any disease. She said I probably felt humbled, and that is exactly it. I was humbled and ashamed. I felt like a failure.

She also brought up the idea that women need to start praying for men! What if every woman started praying for the men of America, that they'd truly be men of God, and leaders in homes? They have so much temptation these days, especially since they are visually stimulated. I mean, they can't even go to the grocery store without being bombarded in the checkout line with magazine covers showing women wearing very little. Some of these are women's magazines, which puzzles me. Who really buys these? But I digress. Sexual messages are blaring in our own living rooms and cars through the television and radio. There is the obvious problem with pornography via the internet. I often listen to talk radio during my lunchtime (which may indicate I'm getting old). The show I listen to is *New Life*, [53] which is a great show of Christian counselors who give wise advice. In the past I remember many women callers talking about how they'd caught their husband viewing pornography on the internet. It is an epidemic! And I believe women really need to take a hard look at ourselves. How are we dressing? If we are going to church, but are dressing provocatively causing the man behind us to stumble, are we really worshiping God? And how are we teaching our daughters to dress? I'm not suggesting we wear turtlenecks and long skirts dragging the ground, but that we dress attractively and modestly.

Thursday, March 30, 2006 8:35 pm

This morning I was working away at the office when my mom called and says, "Didn't I tell you one day you were going to be a motivational speaker?" I said, "Uh, yes, but that is because you are my mom." She then said, "Has Angie called you?" Side note: Angie's mom and my mom were best friends for many years. My mom was her maid of honor when she married Jim, and after her death, my mom eventually married Jim – thus Angie's stepfather is also my stepfather. (Yep, we pretty much put the fun in the "dysfunctional family". Ha Ha) Anyway, I haven't seen Angie since August at a surprise birthday party for our step dad. I said to my mom, "No. Why would Angie call me?" I like Angie, don't get me wrong. We just aren't close. I knew she was also going through a divorce and was having a very hard time with it this summer. I offered to talk with her if she ever needed that. So my mom said, "Oh, I can't tell you, but she has a good story for you." I said to my mom, "Oh no, you can't call me and leave me hangin' with that!" So she spilled the beans but made me promise to act surprised if Angie called me. (Now I think I have it in writing my mom wants me to actually lie!) Here is a cool story of only God's doing.

Angie decided to go to a counselor who just happens to be Tina, the one who I had been going to off and on for several years, before my husband left, just to guide me on blended family issues. Tina is the one who called a few days ago (on March 20). One of the things we talked about during the phone call was me giving my talk at the girls' retreat. Tina asked if she could have a copy so I put one in the mail the next day and forgot all about it.

Back to Angie. She is hurting, so Tina read her something that "one of her patients wrote." She read *my* talk to Angie. When she was finished reading it, Angie realized it was written by me since she knows my girls and me. She called my mom and asked for my phone number so she could call me.

Is God incredible or what? On New Years Day, I wrote this message I just feel God put on my heart for the girls retreat, but at the end of March, He uses it to speak hope to a hurting woman going through a divorce who just happens to be my sort-of stepsister! The night this was unfolding, I was sitting in my cuddle chair watching The Amazing Race on TV while snacking on chocolate chip cookie dough. God was behind the scenes orchestrating a cool situation and using me (unbeknownst to me at that time). Yep, I believe God is always working in our lives, even when we don't know it.

Lord, Angie may call me, and I am thankful for this "heads up" so I can begin to pray for Your wisdom and words to say to her. She is hurting and I want for her to have the peace, contentment and relationship with You that I have. So, I am Yours. Please keep me from saying anything stupid (I do that a lot) or anything You would not have me say. Lord, I'd love for her to come to our women's Bible study. (Note: In 2009 Angie attended a class with me.)

My mom ends our call by again saying, "See you're already a speaker – you've already motivated someone." She is kind, and a little prejudiced as moms tend to be. (I love her.) I say God is the speaker and I am just the microphone He used to get His message out. What an honor to be used by Him.

Monday, April 3, 2006

Yesterday I started reading, *God Will Make A Way* by Henry Cloud and Steve Auterburn.[19] Although I admire the authors I really had no intention of reading it, but a friend of a friend had given it to me months ago. He heard what I was going through because he'd been through a divorce several years ago himself. I wanted to be able to return it and say in all honesty that I had read it. Well, it is great! I thought since I already knew God will make a way for me, I didn't need to read it. I am so glad I changed my mind. I can't wait to continue so I can glean more insights.

Yesterday I read this, *"We need to get active in seeking God's purposes and dreams for us. Dreams that come from God are never based in wrong or selfish motives. Only if they are based in good motives are they truly God's dreams for us, and in that case we can count on Him to make a way for them to come to fruition. If a dream comes from God, through our heart, He will make a way for it to be realized."*[20] Wow oh wow! I love this. This seems to suggest my dream of writing a book, and maybe even speaking, may be dreams from God, as I truly only have two motivations: 1) to help and encourage others who have been through separation and divorce, and 2) to give glory to

God by showing how He has healed my heart and life, and encourage them that He longs to do the same for them.

So Lord, help me to not get in Your way. Help me to do all I need to do to make these dreams a reality. Actually, it would be You who makes them a reality, but show me each step You want me to take.

Lord, thank You for the blessings You shower on me – my daughters, my friends and family, health, job, home, car, etc. Thank You that the Fern Creek Christian team is safely in New Orleans, and be with each of them as they serve the hurricane victims there. Please keep them safe and healthy and remind them that they are there as Your ambassadors.

VIII

Loneliness

Saturday, April 8, 2006

I've felt lonely the last couple of days. I came home from the Gospel Music Awards to an empty house. It was the same yesterday because Nickie is in New Orleans, Katie is in Cincinnati, and Gina is in Mexico. I cried as I kneeled to pray last night, but I know I am not alone – God is always with me! Then I thought how Christ has been alone – totally alone on the cross. God, who is holy and cannot be in the presence of sin, could not even look at Him as He hung on the cross, as my sins and the sins of the world were on Him. Totally alone! Oh how Christ knows how I feel! I was encouraged by that, but also saddened that He, my Savior, who was without sin, had to endure the beatings and the mocking and the excruciating pain of being crucified for my sake. But His love for me and for all humanity held Him on that cross. You see, He had a purpose, and He knew what it was, and He carried it out. Praise Him!

I guess I thought since I've been doing well, there would be no more tears or feelings of abandonment or aloneness. But our lives are filled with pain. God even tells us in the Bible, (John 16:33) "*In this world, you* ***will*** *have troubles.*" It is how we decide to deal with the pain that will shape us, and our future. I pray that each day God will show me His will for me. I know He promises an abundant life.

Help me, Lord, to not pity myself but instead search Your word and be still and listen for Your wisdom. Help me to remember to invite You into my quiet time each day. Please speak to me. Help me to do all You want me to. Thank you for your promise that You have a plan in place for me, You plan to prosper me and give me an abundant life, just as You promised in Jeremiah 29:11. Help me to help others in my shoes, Lord. I know in order to do that well, I must go through the same emotions (sadness, abandonment, loneliness, rejection) so I can be more effective and so they will see that You, Lord, have been with me and healed my heart and You long to do the same for them. I have so many friends, Lord, and I treasure them and praise You for giving them to me. Help me to know it is OK to be weak at times and to call on them if I need to. Help me feel Your presence and never doubt Your love or plan for me when something doesn't happen as I think it should.

Today I read an article in the Southeast Christian Outlook Newspaper by John Faust. It said, "While uncomfortable, the temporary suffering we go through in this life can create opportunities to help others grow in Christian faith and contribute to God's purpose of reconciling people to Himself for eternity. Only He knows how all this will play out. We must trust Him. If we focus less on ourselves and more on God's ultimate will, we will be on the right road of learning how to 'be joyful always and give thanks in all circumstances,'" (I Thes. 5:16-17). God knows what's around the corner. We do not. Let's humbly ask Him for directions and follow His leading. This has been my prayer!

Monday, April 10, 2006

Today Jenny, a petite 75-year old woman who works in my office building, saw me in the hall and asked if "I'd met a man friend yet." I told her it has only been about 14 months since my husband left, so I am not yet in the right frame of mind to make wise decisions. I'm afraid I'd just like the idea of not being alone and would go out with just anyone. I believe I'm exactly where God wants me to be, so I can better focus on Him and what He wants me to do (like write the book). She said, "Well, you are young and beautiful and I think God has someone for you." Wow – I don't remember being told I was beautiful before so that was so encouraging (plus she is a wise woman). What a blessing a few encouraging words can be!

Friday, April 14, 2006

Last night, I attended the first week of a new video Bible study at church called "The Patriarchs" by Beth Moore. [21] It will be a deep study about our roots as Christians, and I am so excited about it. I am at a place in my life where I am hungry to know more about God and His mysterious ways, and I pray that I will never lose this desire to know Him more. Beth Moore has been a role model for me from the first time I heard her speak about 6 years ago. She came out on stage and literally got on her knees as she led thousands of us in corporate prayer! I'd never seen that done, and it brought tears to my eyes. To see a woman so in love with God was amazing to me, and I remember thinking, "Now that is the relationship with God for which I long." At that time I didn't realize what that sort of love relationship would require, but as I've gone through "the valley" during the last year, I now know it takes pain, trust, complete brokenness and dependence on Him. I would never want to re-live what I have gone through, and I don't want to encourage anyone to go out and seek "the valley" but I am so thankful God is faithful to me, and to you . . . even in the valley times of life. He truly has a plan for each of us, and if we will draw close to Him, He will be faithful to guide us each day. It would be great if we'd learn to search Him and stay close to Him always and not need a "valley" experience to get our attention.

Last night on the video, Beth said, "It is no accident you are here." She also explained that the greatest story ever told is the story of Christ. She is so right, but then she said, "Our lives are also meant to be a great story and easy lives don't make great stories. We'd put a book like that down after the second chapter."[22] Wow, I just felt she was speaking directly to me, especially when she mentioned a book. My prayer has been for God to use me, and what I've learned, to help others.

My favorite stories are ones of people helping people. I can't help but think of a couple of mission trips I've been on and how when we'd get back we'd tell our congregation of the great things that happened as we were helping people. I can't think of a prouder moment than when I heard my own daughters talk of their experiences doing this. (Sort of confirms I've done something right in raising them.) Katie literally dug a ditch for a future sewer line in the hot Mexico sun for two days and had numerous blisters on her hands. She will never know how many people her efforts touched, but she can know she did something to help others in the name of Christ. Nickie rocked a toddler with numerous medical problems in an orphanage in Honduras for hours. (I think she wanted to sneak her home in her suitcase.) This seems like such a small thing, but for several hours that little girl knew someone cared for her. I can't help but think of Mother Theresa. Now there is a great story! What a woman! What a beautiful spirit, because all she did, she did for the glory of Christ. She allowed Him to live through her. I can't imagine the smile on her face, now, as she is surely in heaven with Him, her Savior!

Last night's study focused on names and how important they are to us, and how we want our name to be remembered. We need to really shed this human-desire and live in a way to where Jesus' name is remembered. In my city, Southeast Christian Church puts on an incredible Broadway-style Easter Pageant. I would say there are at least 1,500 volunteers who work on this for months, from building the stages, to writing and rehearsing the music to selling tickets, etc. It is a magnificent performance and has spoken to thousands over the years, but the program doesn't list any names. This is because these people want only one name remembered – the only name that matters – Jesus Christ. Amazing! These people are so in love with Christ and are so thankful for His sacrifice and love for them that they only want the audience to know Him more or to meet Him for the first time through their performance (and they put on 12 in a two-week period). I feel certain God remembers their names – what a humbling but remarkable thought.

Remarriage

In *God Will Make A Way*, one of the authors explains how important it is to really look at yourself and heal during times of being single. He says, "... you have the opportunity to discover the richness of life apart from marriage. Life is more than marriage. God intended us to find a relationship with Him, a community of safe people, some meaningful tasks, and a mission and purpose in order to have a good life on this earth. Marriage is one of the best experiences in this life. However, marriage is not life. It is a part of life. And for many, life does not ever include marriage." [23] Wow, I needed to hear that and now I need to remember it.

It seems strange to me after two failed marriages, I would even desire it again. I mean am I just a glutton for punishment? I think God has made us to be relational beings (some of us more than others) and especially women, He made to be romantics. We want to be loved and cherished. Speaking for myself, I just love the idea of having someone think I am the best thing since sliced bread; someone who they can't wait to tell me good news, or want to hug me when they see me. Someone who when they see me can't help but smile because they are so happy. Someone who thinks I am beautiful (on the inside and on the outside). Yep, I am definitely a romantic. But so is God – have you ever read Song of Songs! The Creator of the Universe actually looks down at me and sees a beautiful child of God. He longs to hear me pray and thank Him for His goodness, mercy and blessings. He longs to give me gifts, too. (And who doesn't like that?) This does not mean I am perfect, by any means, but He knows my heart and my heart's desires, and if I am faithful to follow Him, to search His will for my life, our desires will mesh and He will allow them to become a reality. If I come to know Him, my desires will no longer be about me, but about how I can live my life for Him. And there really is no greater place to be than right smack in the middle of God's will.

Now that I've said that, I know instead of focusing on being married again some day, I need to focus on God's word (my relationship with Him), I need to stay involved in my church family (community), I need to continue to heal and to discover both the positive and negative traits I brought into both of my previous marriages. I need to continue to pray my "big prayers" for God's will in my life and persist in writing this book (tasks and mission).

Saturday, April 15, 2006

Last night I attended the Good Friday service at church and it was a really nice, reflective service. I felt since I was given the day off work, I wanted to be sure I focused on what happened over 2,000 years ago. Jesus willingly gave up his life for me! It is incomprehensible, actually. During the service, a portion of "The Passion of The Christ" [24] was shown where Barabbas is released and there is a close-up of the actor portraying Jesus, who had been whipped. His face was bruised and cut, and it hit me, "What right do I have to pray for a happy life?"

Was Jesus happy when He was on earth? He was here solely to do His Father's will . . . which ultimately led to dying for our sins. Maybe He wasn't happy, but I bet He experienced some **joy** here, especially when His followers showed their faith in Him. When Peter got out of the boat, when the little children ran to him, when He healed the lepers and one returned to thank Him, when He saw the widow give all she had, when John the Beloved would actually lean against him as they ate, and especially when his Father said, "This is My Son in whom I am well pleased." I wonder if He still feels that same joy when we put our faith in Him, when someone is baptized in His name. He is in heaven with God, so there has to be amazing joy there. We have the promise of joining Him there some day to experience "paradise," where there are no more tears. (I like the sound of this, although sometimes I wonder if I have any more to shed.) I need to be sure I pray for a joy-filled life, which if I am doing His will, how can I experience any other emotion?

Friday, April 21, 2006

Beth Moore's Bible study[25] last night mentioned that even the people who we think have it all together (such as speakers and musical artists) are still afraid, but they are more afraid of not doing God's will then being afraid of failing. Even though they are afraid or nervous, they go on and God must be pleased with their obedience and trust and faith in Him. I need to remember this whenever I am afraid or nervous. In the Bible, Revelation 20:12 says, "*I saw the dead, both great and small, standing before God's throne. And the books were open, including the Book of Life. And the dead were judged according to what they had done, as recorded in the books.*" I'm no scholar and I'm not sure how all of this will play out, so for now I will focus on using the gifts God has given me even when I'm uncertain. Help me, Jesus!

And speaking of fear, I learned recently that "Do not be afraid" and "Fear not" are the most repeated commands in the Bible. I think God knew fear could be a major stumbling block for us. In fact, I've learned this idea is stated 365 times in the Bible . . . that is one time for each day of the year. God knows us well!

Thursday, April 27, 2006

Today I had lunch with Chase, my accountant friend, and she shared the happy news she is going to have a baby! She is so encouraging to me and told me I have actually ministered to her, even though she isn't in my shoes. She thinks my book will be a blessing to others and I do a great job of keeping the focus on God.

So Lord, thank you for that affirmation. Please continue to be with me each and every day and use me for Your glory and honor. I want the focus to be on how You have been with me, helped me, and how You long to do the same for others. You are God – nothing is too difficult for You. Praise You!

Tonight I had dinner with another friend who is separated from her husband. *Please give me your wisdom and words, Lord, as we continue sharing our stories. I don't want her for one second to think I rejoice in divorce, because I absolutely hate it and what it does to all involved. But if her husband is not going to change and continues to be unfaithful, it is OK for her to move on, to seek counseling, and to heal. Help her to know You will bless her and You do have a plan for her. Help me to be the friend she needs.*

Angie and I went to Bible study and it was so good. I enjoy it so much! I am like a sponge absorbing it all in. Tonight Ann, our facilitator, mentioned she loves it when I sing at church. Wow – what a nice surprise!

In the video[26], Beth Moore talked about how her husband feels God leading him to pray for all the women who do not have a husband; to pray over them. How cool is that!

I love how she said God would not have given her husband this leading if He were not going to listen! So prayer (especially intercessory) is a wonderful and powerful thing.

Lord, thank You for all You have done for me. I have been abundantly blessed! If I did not receive another, I am already overflowing! But I know I will because You long to give your children good gifts. So thank You in advance as I trust the plans You have for me will include an abundant life. Help me to keep in Your word and to learn all You have for me. Help me to grow even more in my passion to know You! I truly want You to be the love of my life!

Tuesday, May 2, 2006

Tonight I watched as Nickie received her National Honor Society cords. It seems like yesterday when I was in that very spot watching her as a sophomore being inducted into NHS. The time has flown! I am so proud of her, of her academic accomplishments, but even more so for her character. Lord, thank You for my wonderful daughters – I love them with my whole heart!

So many thoughts have been going through my limited brain today. The sky today was cloudy with these big puffy clouds, and the sun shone through looking like heaven's own rays were touching the earth. It felt like a smile from God. A little later, it would threaten rain and I envisioned myself out in the rain with my face and hands towards the heavens as if the very raindrops themselves represented the blessings that God continually pours on me. Then I thought, "Why don't I try that sometime – just stand in the rain and praise God for it? Why am I always so practical and run indoors to escape getting wet?" Maybe this new chapter in my life will allow me to be more carefree – not careless, but a little more relaxed and spontaneous – allowing me to enjoy some interruptions.

God, You are amazing! I am overflowing with gratitude, love and delight for You! Help me continue those feelings for You always! Please continue to help me know Your will and help me be more like You.

Saturday, May 06, 2006

Today in my Bible study, [26] the first question was, "What is God called in Romans 15:13?" The answer is, "The God of Hope." Hello! I love that for so many reasons. Obviously if I don't have hope for the future – that God will work His plan out for me, then life would not be worth living – sort of what mom meant, I think, when she said I'd given Angie hope. One of the first questions Angie asked was, "So is there life after divorce?" She needed to hear from someone who had recently gone through it that, Yes, there definitely is! There is hope!

Another part of the study talked about beauty, and this brought tears to my eyes. Will a man ever think I'm beautiful? There are so many gorgeous women out there who turn men's heads, and I am definitely not one of them. Now I don't think I'm dog-ugly or anything, and I have never felt more confident as I do now (probably because I've never been closer to God), so this part of the lesson made me feel better, as Beth Moore said, "As you stare into your Bible and take in what He says, the light of God's word reflects off your face and you become radiant."[27] Wow – I love that! After all, I truly want a man whose heart matches mine – radiant with God's word – who seeks God and His will for his life.

Monday, May 8, 2006

I was listening to a Chris Tomlin CD (shocker) and the song with these lyrics came on: "Only things that satisfy come from You. Everything that's beautiful, that's wonderful . . . Your hope, Your love, Your peace . . ."[28] I needed to hear that. *God, please help me to focus mostly on inner beauty by keeping in Your word – I want to radiate You.*

In today's Bible study, I learned sometimes God answers our prayer before we even get the request out of our mouth. I'd never thought of that before. Wow. *So just by going with my instinct, I feel You are saying "yes" to the book dream, and "yes" to the speaking dream.* Also in today's lesson I learned Abraham's servant prayed a specific prayer. He prayed the chosen woman would say, "May I water your camels too." (Apparently in that day, that was something highly unlikely to happen.) *He prayed for this sign from You as he knew You are God of the impossible . . . not the God of the improbable.*[29] *Praise You! Help me to be so bold!*

Tuesday, May 9, 2006

On Sunday night, I attended my last youth group parent meeting at church, and it hit me hard. I ended up crying when I got home feeling as though my life was over. I've been a mom for almost 20 years and my girls are nearly grown and will soon be out on their own. Thankfully, Gina was home and let me cry and talk (and eat ice cream right out of the carton). I said to her, "What if God really doesn't have any other plan for me? What if this is all He wanted me to do?" But I know in my heart this isn't true. I felt like the man in the Bible who said he believed but in the very next sentence said, "Lord, help my unbelief." Yep, that was me.

I talked to my phone counselor, Debbie, yesterday, and told her I think part of my sad emotions lately are again due to grieving a dream. In the past, whenever, I thought about Katie and Nickie grown and out on their own, I also thought I'd have a spouse to celebrate their accomplishments with and to do fun things with as a couple. I never saw myself alone at this point in my life. I have thought of Brady, since he was a part of the girls' growing up years, and how he'd be proud of them. I don't think I miss him anymore – I miss the dream of having someone special with me sharing in these life events. Debbie assured me it is only natural to feel these emotions and to give them to God – tears and all. (Lord, do you have a bucket-full yet?) I know if I don't go through the grieving process, I won't truly heal. So I know I have some tough days ahead.

Lord, I pray you'll be with me, Katie and Nickie, and help us to rejoice at their accomplishments. Please be near me and forgive my unbelief. I know You can do anything. I sometimes think I won't pick up on Your plan and will miss it. In one of my Bible study lessons, Beth Moore hit my thoughts on the head. She said, "All of us long for God to make His will crystal clear." Yep, that's me! But maybe since that doesn't take faith, You don't work that way?

IX

Life Is Like A Book

Our lives are like a book. Sometimes chapters feel like a mystery or a soap opera. Sometimes we wish parts of them were fictitious. Some chapters are even inspirational (thank God). Some are fun to live and then to "re-read" as we reminisce with family or friends. Some chapters are longer than others. Some chapters of our lives are slammed shut on us suddenly and filled with pain and grief. Some chapters we go back over so many times the pages are yellowed and dog-eared with regret and "what ifs".

Sometimes in a good book, especially if we have grown fond of the characters, we want to peek at the end of the story to be assured they are OK or even that they win. In our story of life, thankfully, if we have accepted Jesus as our Savior, we already can be assured of our ending . . . and we win! After we have drawn our last breath on earth, we are promised a permanent home in heaven. The Bible says, "*to be absent from the body is to be present with the Lord.*" Christ said,

"*I will go to prepare a place for you and if I prepare a place for you, I will come back for you.*" (John 14: 2-3).

Since God has taken care of the ending for us, we need to spend our energy writing the chapters of our lives carefully, in a way where the generations that follow will want to hear our stories, and learn from them and pass on the good stuff.

Sunday, May 21, 2006

Today my friend, Christy and I sang at church, and it went really well. We sang Avalon's "Orphan of God." [30] We didn't even get to practice together until 8:45 a.m. and the first service started at 9:15 a.m. So praise be to God, it went well and we received numerous compliments when it was over. I remember for the first time ever thinking in the middle of the song, "Hey, this is fun!" I was nervous as always, but not quite as nervous as I usually get, so thank You, God, for taking some of those nerves away. I remember thinking all week there really is no reason to be so nervous because I am really singing to God. He has heard me practice about a bazillion times, so if I mess up, He really won't care. **He'll just be pleased with my efforts and my willingness to use a talent He gave me in spite of my nervousness and fear**. I love to sing, and I want to ensure He doesn't take this gift from me, so I need to use it whenever I can and be sure to give Him thanks for this gift. I have to admit it felt so good when people told us we did a good job. A couple even said we did a "phenomenal" job, so how cool is that? I'd been praying that week I would not focus on desiring the praises of men (and women), but God allowed some to praise us anyway.

Friday, May 26, 2006

Today I went to Seneca High School's graduation to celebrate six of my Sunday school students' graduation. I almost teared-up as the "Pomp and Circumstance" song played realizing that next Friday, I'd be watching my very own "baby" graduate from high school. I'm hoping I'll be able to keep the tears at bay during the ceremony and enjoy it for her.

Tomorrow I have several graduation parties to attend, and I'm sort of nervous about it. To go alone will be difficult, so I'm hoping Katie or Nickie will go with me. I don't mean to be so fragile, but this has been a really hard season for me.

Lord, help me not to focus on being alone – help me instead to focus on all You have done for me. No one has everything; and about the only thing I don't have is a husband or significant other. I am sorry when I focus on the one thing I don't have. I am going to try to focus on all You have given me: my health, my daughters and their health, my home, my new car, my incredible job and co-workers, my loving church family, my family, my friends, my salvation, Your love, and a hope for the future.

I love You and continue to pray I'll discover Your perfect will for my life. Amen.

Saturday, May 27, 2006

Today was another emotional day for me. I woke up crying. I figured out going to the graduation parties will be difficult for me because the last time I visited these people's homes was with Brady. Although both of these families know of the divorce, no one has said a word to me about it. That is no fault of theirs. I mean, who really knows what to say in such a situation? It is sort of uncomfortable . . . like having a big elephant in the room and everyone just walks around it. I had every intention of going, as the students mean a lot to me and I'd do anything for them, but I remembered my counselor said it was OK to take care of myself, so I chose not to go as I just knew I'd cry. And how much fun would that be at a celebration?

I have cried several times today at home. The deep hurt of being rejected came back to me so strongly. Maybe it was due to actually going to the graduation yesterday and being the only single adult among my friends there. Maybe it is in combination with realizing next week Nickie will graduate and soon thereafter she'll leave for college. Anyway, I realized if I'm actually going to help those in these painful divorce shoes, I need to share that even a year and a half after my husband left, some days we are just going to hurt and that is normal. It is understandable. We loved our spouses deeply, so it is only natural to hurt when we have been rejected. This person has been part of our every day life for several years, so to not hurt would not be natural. **We need to be careful to not fill our lives so full of activities we are too busy to experience the pain. Only in this pain can we truly experience the healing of God.**

Lord, thank You for being with me today, even in my pain. I know You do not enjoy seeing me cry and ache, but I believe You are most pleased with me when even then, in the midst of my hurting heart and unanswered questions, I trust in You and don't give up. I don't know the timing of Your plan for me, but do believe You are working out all the details and that in Your perfect timing your incredible plan for my future will be revealed. Again, help me not to miss anything You want me to do or learn. Help me to stay out of your way. You are

God! If You can put all the stars in place and keep the earth on its axis for all these years, You can certainly work out any and all details of my life without my help, for heaven's sake. Thank You for getting me through the day. Amen.

I propose . . .

Thinking back on both of my marriage proposals, neither man got down on one knee to ask me to marry him. Could this have been an outward sign of their hearts? Could my acceptance been a sign of my desperation? In marriage we are called to serve each other. If the man cannot even get down on one knee when proposing to the "woman of his dreams," what does that say about him? What does it say about the woman to whom he is proposing? Did either man really cherish me or the idea of being there for and with me 'til death do us part?

We women are such romantics, so we just love to hear a tender proposal story. As soon as we see the engagement ring and finish our oohing and aahing, don't we immediately ask, "How did he propose?"

Sadly, some of us have such low self-esteem we don't think ourselves worthy of such a proposal. We are just happy someone, anyone, has asked us to marry him. If we have any foreshadowing of some lack of character, we believe we can change that after the wedding. Oh, but to have a man so crazy for me he would be more than willing (in fact he'd think it an honor) to get down on his knee in a vulnerable and servant-like position, and with all his heart desire to spend the rest of his life with me. He might even be a little nervous as to my answer, but so hoping and trusting that

I'll say yes. (Yep, I'm a romantic at heart. Watch for a fiction romance novel coming soon. Ha Ha)

Some men even come up with elaborate plans. How wonderful and honoring for the woman to know he finds her so irresistible and worthy he has worked hard to set everything up just to ask her to marry him. Wow, would this in itself be some foreshadowing of his treatment of his bride?

As I write this, I can't help but think about the correlation of a man proposing, getting down on his knee, and how we are to get down on our knees when we pray. This action says total surrender. It puts us in a vulnerable position. It says, "I am Your servant and I honor You."

I am not saying our husbands are to be our servants (unless they want to – ha ha). But I believe with all my heart that both spouses are to serve each other. But ladies, even if you are single, I want you to know a man has gotten down on his knee for you because he felt you are worthy. It was under the weight of a cross. The cross was heavy. Our sin was heavy, but Jesus loved us so much that He stumbled under the weight – under the weight of His love for us. He then willingly gave up His very own life for us, for our forgiveness and reconciliation to the Father, the perfect God of the universe.

So if we have never gotten a proper proposal, know there is one man who wooed you, who is still wooing you. One who not only promised to die for you, but one who actually did so. But Christ didn't say, 'til death do us part,' because when we die our physical death someday, our Bridegroom will be waiting for us in Heaven. He will welcome us with open arms and nail-scarred hands, and we will get to spend eternity with Him. I just know there will be an amazing wedding feast and reception that day. (Personally I'm hoping for a chocolate wedding cake.)

In anticipation, I want to live a life worthy of His love; a life that will be a foreshadowing of **my** character. I want to be spotless and wear white! And I want Him to be so pleased with me that when He sees me in my dress and veil of white, He will be excited, awaiting my arrival.

Praise you, Lord, for your love, grace, patience and endless love. What a model You are of how we all should treat others – dying to our self and our desires. I am pretty sure You didn't want to die but You wanted more than anything to do Your Father's will, so that is my prayer too. Help me to know Your perfect will for my life. Help me as I believe I am right where You want me now and to be patient as you are molding me and working out Your plan, even though I can't see it clearly now. I do totally trust you, God, as I have no doubt that You are in control, and I praise You for that.

Sunday, June 11, 2006

So this week, the word "reign" and "rain" have really been on my mind. I am praying God will tell me exactly what He wants me to write regarding these. Today in church, we sang the song entitled, "*Shine Jesus Shine*" as our closing hymn. At the beginning of the service, we sang a song that included the word "reign." This word just hit me in the face because each day for the last several days when I'd turn on the radio, a song with that word in the lyrics would be on and it would catch my attention.

In church today I prayed Christ would truly reign in me – that His sovereign authority would rule my every thought and action and decision. *I pray, Lord, reign in me. Soak me to the bone with Your wisdom, love, peace, joy, patience and goodness. Then I will have no choice but to exude Your love and goodness, my heart's desire.*

I thought, when it rains, the sun isn't usually shining. But with God reigning on us, the Son is definitely shining. So like the song we sang this morning says, Shine Jesus Shine! Shine on me and through me. Like the sun kisses our skin with a pink glow after we've been exposed to it, please kiss us, as when we have truly been touched by You, our appearance should change too. We will have the most radiant smile and hope-filled eyes and when the Son touches you, you will not be burned. When we Son-worship, there is no danger as only good and praiseworthy and beautiful things come from being exposed to Him. In fact the only danger is when we are not exposed to the Son . . . some serious burns could then occur.

Lord, thank You for healing me and teaching me. Thank You for using this pain-filled part of my life to heal me and to draw me closer to You, my first love. Lord, I never want to be far from You. Help me always to remember that even when I go through times in my life when I can't see You working, help me to know You are always at work – fine-tuning details to make Your plan come to fruition. I can't help but think of I Corinthians 2:9, "No eye has seen, no ear has heard, no man has conceived what God has prepared for those who love him." Wow, what a promise! I can't wait!

Saturday, June 17, 2006

I woke up early this morning with the following thoughts running through my head:

Like flowers need the sun and rain to break out of their hard seedling shell and bloom to be what they were intended to be, we need the Son to reign on us, to soak us to the bones with His love, peace, comfort and grace. When we truly trust and put our lives and situations in His hands, He can bring about the most beautiful hearts and from the overflow of the heart, the mouth speaks. Oh may we speak of what He has done for us!

To be a beautiful flower in God's garden and stand up tall (well, as tall as we can, thank you very much) and proud and long for His radiance – a Son-kissed face. There is nothing more beautiful than when we radiate Him.

Sunday, June 18, 2006

Yesterday I went to the Ichthus Christian Music Festival in Wilmore, Kentucky with Nickie to see my favorite artist, Chris Tomlin, and others. We arrived around 6:30 p.m. and were able to take part in a communion service with 17,000 other brothers and sisters in Christ. It was so touching that a couple of tears escaped my eyes and ran down my cheeks. The weather was very warm when we arrived but by about 7:45 p.m. I remember sitting on our blanket awaiting Chris Tomlin to take the stage. The temperature was perfect and there was a gentle breeze blowing through my hair. I just sat there and **savored the moment**. There was no place I'd rather be. How fun to experience this with one of my daughters! When Chris Tomlin got on stage and started singing, I went up closer and sang along for the whole hour. He did a great job and ended with "How Great Thou Art" with him and the band quietly leaving the stage while the crowd continued to worship. They wanted the last sounds to be that of the people worshiping God, not clapping for them! Amazing. There was that worship-filled heart that came out in his book that so touched my heart. It was an incredible night.

Tuesday, June 20, 2006

Driving to work this morning, it was raining but the sun was shining. At one point on my journey I drove down a hill and saw the bright sun shining through a downpour of rain! I smiled and laughed out loud as I thought about what I'd written a couple of days ago. And if I had not been on my way to work in my business suit and high-heels, I would have gotten out of my car to let that soothing rain soak me through and through in the sun's light.

What a vision in my head – how freeing not to care what anyone thought but just to twirl around in the rain giggling like a little girl as I basked in my Father's outpouring of healing rain.

Wednesday, June 21, 2006

Tonight after vocal team practice, Steve, who will be leading worship this week, talked about **expectancy** – what would happen if every Sunday when we walked into the sanctuary we were expecting You to be there and for hearts to be moved! How would our attitudes be different? How would I hold myself if I expected to encounter You, the King of Glory, in my midst? How reverent would I be, knowing You were there waiting to be praised and honored?

Lord, help me to change and be more like this everyday. I believe You show Yourself in unexpected places, at unexpected times, so help me to search and watch for You and expect You each day. In my quiet time help me to not just go through the motions but to instead expect and invite You in. Lord, I am speechless at Your goodness. Thank You for being so real to me, for giving me peace and joy. I hope I can exude that to others.

Lord, today I got to thinking I have no right to ask You for anything and my happiness is not the most important thing in the world. What is important is living in obedience to You in the hopes that others will be drawn to You. So help me to remember that. I love You so, Lord, and praise You and thank You for who You are and how You have wooed me to Yourself.

Thursday, June 22, 2006

Tonight was our last Bible Study. It has been an inspiring study and I am so grateful I was able to be part of it. Here are some notes from it that especially spoke to me:

Remember **endings are not all bad because a new beginning will be starting**. For me this has been evident from my divorce. I did not want the marriage to end, and it was extremely painful. But God, through His amazing goodness and grace, has given me a new beginning. I long to live the rest of my days serving Him and finding out what His perfect plan for me is here on earth. Another way this is in play in my life is that Nickie just graduated from high school. For her, there is an ending and a beginning of going away to college. For me, it is the ending of having my daughter at home living with me, but it is the beginning of her making adult choices and planning for her future. It is a bittersweet time for both of us. We will both have more freedom, and I can't help but wonder how God will use this "free time" of mine to serve Him.

In Genesis 50:20, Joseph said to his brothers, "*You intended to harm me, but God intended it for good . . .* " I think this is true of my divorce. I doubt my husband knew how devastating it would be for me when he walked out, but I can't help but think if he was really concerned about my feelings, he would have talked to me and shared he felt we needed to separate and work on things instead of just leaving and not giving me any say in the matter. To be rejected by your spouse is one of the most painful experiences we can face. But once again, God has come to my rescue. No, He didn't rescue me by taking the pain away, instead He allowed me to hurt and to grieve and heal, but He did not leave me for one second. He has taught me to depend on Him. He has given me a peace I can't explain, and I believe in my heart He will use this situation to bring glory to His name. He is allowing me to share my story with others and bring them hope that what He has so lovingly done for me He wants to do for them!

Today on my way home from work, author and speaker, Luci Swindoll, was speaking on the radio. I've heard her before at several Women of Faith conferences and she does a remarkable job. The first thing I heard her say was, **"Life is what you make it."** Wow! Then she talked about celebrating often. Another piece of wisdom she shared was to "**savor the moment.**" Oh how I love that idea! I need to work on this; however, for some reason, I did do this Saturday at Ichthus. Our lives are so fast-paced and it is so hard to do this, so Lord, help me to slow down and savor lots of moments. Then she talked about taking risks . . . even though it is risky. So often I think to myself, "What if I fail, what if I humiliate myself?" But I don't want to have a lot of "what ifs" and regrets on my deathbed. Lord, help me to not be foolish, but to walk by faith so if You want me to take a risk, I'll do so fearlessly!

She talked about how she was asked to write a book about the single life and, although it was a risk, she took it. It has opened so many doors for her. As I drove, I couldn't help but think about my book as I still think this idea is from You, Lord. Praise You!

Unloved?

It is horrible to feel unloved as a wife. In Proverbs 30: 21, it says, "*Under three things the earth trembles* . . . (and one of these is) *an unloved woman who is married.*" I know the feeling. I've been there . . . twice. And I'm not unlovable at all. I just chose men who chose to love themselves rather than me. They told me they loved me, and because I longed to hear those words, I believed them. Maybe they thought they did, but when things got tough with raising children or with financial pressures, they did not choose to stick it out with faith that God would work it all out. They chose to leave me and the girls and a relationship I believe God would have blessed if they would have honored their wedding day commitment. You see, anyone can speak the words, but it takes a special person to truly mean it, and more importantly, live it.

To **truly love is to make a conscience choice** to honor a person each day. Love is not a mushy feeling – it is a choice. And I am glad. People's feelings change all the time. We feel tired or sad or happy, etc. But when we tell someone we love them, we are really saying, "I am making a choice to love you today." Can you image the mother of a newborn baby who loved only based on her feelings at the moment? Who really feels like getting up every two hours to feed them or change a diaper in the middle of the night?

But mothers make a choice to do so because they love their child and this is one of the ways they show it.

As I look back, I didn't consciously think I was unloved, but I think deep in my soul I suspected as much. My husband made a choice to not bother to be at the hospital when I had my gallbladder removed (and I was scared) and this choice hurt my feelings. I never realized this was an outward sign of his hard heart, of his un-love for me.

But I need to share in the blame in this situation. I should have told him I wanted him there. . . that I **needed** him there. But I was afraid he'd get mad; I didn't want to be a bother to him, so I kept the hurt and disappointment inside. In hindsight, maybe he needed to hear I needed him.

I think choices such as these hurt God deeply too. I know when someone hurts one of my children, I hurt for them and sometimes want to get even! (If you are a mother, you know exactly what I am talking about, don't you?) God has a really tough job because, although He hurt for me, his child who was being treated unfairly, He also hurt because one of his other children did the hurting and is probably hurting himself. I can almost picture God saying, "Come back to me, child. Get rid of that pride and run back into my arms where I will heal you and restore your life." Amazing!

See, we are called to love as Christ loved the church. He did more than just say He loved us. He demonstrated it by dying for us. I'm pretty sure He didn't feel like dying, but He loved God so much He chose to do His will. He was obedient to God's plan. Even on days when we don't feel like loving, we are supposed to be obedient and make the choice to love people. I remember hearing Bob Russell say during one of his sermons years ago about marriage, "We are not called to be happy, we are called to be obedient."

Most likely if you are reading this, you have been an unloved wife. Oh, how my heart breaks for you and I feel that "motherly instinct" of wanting to punch the lights out of the ones who have broken your hearts. (Sorry, I digressed for just a moment.) But I want you to know **you are not unloved. The Creator of the Universe, the King of Kings, loves you with His whole heart. You are precious to Him. He will never stop loving you, no matter what you do or have done**. I urge you to just stop here and truly let that thought, that truth, sink into the core of your being. You'll never be the same once you truly believe this, and live like you do.

A woman in the Bible was also an unloved wife. Her name was Leah, and she was married to Jacob (the son of Isaac). We see in Genesis 29:30 that Jacob "*loved Rachel more than Leah.*" (My heart just aches when I read that verse.) Jacob made a pact to work for Laban (Leah's and Rachel's father and Jacob's uncle) so that Rachel could be his wife. The Bible says in Genesis 29:17 that "*Leah had weak eyes, but Rachel was lovely in form, and beautiful.*" (Whatever! I wish the writer would have told us a little more about Leah, about some of her good and strong traits.) So Laban agrees to this pact. But on the wedding night, Jacob ends up in the marriage bed with Leah, to his surprise. The next morning he confronted his uncle about this "trick" and his response was that it was uncustomary to give the younger daughter in marriage before the older one. So Jacob agreed to work for seven more years to get Rachel. In the meantime, Leah became pregnant. You just need to read the entire story, but in it you'll see Leah keeps trying to earn her husband's love by bearing him children. Finally, by the fourth son's birth, she said in Genesis 29:35 "*This time I will praise the Lord.*"

You go girl! You see, through the years of never getting the approval and love she so desired from her husband, she finally realized she was loved by God, and instead of focusing on what she did not have, she made a choice to focus on the blessings she did have: healthy children and the love of God being at the top of the list.

I relate with Leah on thinking I had to earn love. As I have stated before, I believe it began when I was a child and thought I had to earn my dad's love. I know now this was not the truth, but it was my perception then. It also came from always feeling inferior to my friends who I thought were prettier, more talented, smarter and taller (OK, this last trait was an obvious fact.) In my mind I always came up short (no pun intended) and talked myself into believing my dad would surely rather have one of them for a daughter than some "plain Jane" without any real talent, such as me.

I brought this unhealthy view of love into my marriages, believing if I did almost everything, I could earn my husbands' love. But that is not unconditional love at all, which I'm pretty sure is an important part of marriage. Without that foundation, it shouldn't come as a surprise when my marriages collapsed. Is unconditional love even possible? I mean if someone says I love so-and-so because they love me back, haven't we've just put a condition on the love? I'm not sure we do a very good job with unconditional love because we are bent towards selfishness, thinking what can someone do for us, instead of how can we serve them.

X

Come Running

For some reason I thought today of the night Nickie (at the age of 17) came running to me after being gone on a weeklong mission trip. She was so glad to see me she didn't care if she looked cool or not, or what her friends thought. Her only concern at that moment was being reunited and embracing me. I was so touched by her display of affection, and I will always treasure and savor that moment.

I believe God is like this. **When we show reckless abandon in our love for Him, He is overjoyed**. I think of the story in the Bible of the prodigal son, but we don't have to go to that extreme. We can run to Him even if we just haven't been as close lately. I believe He savors those moments, too. I believe He longs for us to succeed in life; that is actually part of His plan for us. But when we are down, hurt or broken-hearted, He is there for us, too. He is so NOT like us. His love is not conditional on our good works, His love is unconditional . . . He loves us because we are simply His! Wow!

Beauty is in the Eye of the Beholder

I think it is so important for women to know God loves us no matter what we look like on the outside. Our bodies are a temple of the Holy Spirit, and we should take care of ourselves by exercising and eating healthy. But God, our Beholder, sees our hearts and they are beautiful to Him. In our society, almost all of us compare ourselves to the unrealistic images we see on magazine covers, in movies or on television. Sometimes I hate to pass by a mirror or look at a photo of myself, as I know that I'll see my image (duh) but I really want to see Catherine Zeta Jones! (I'm only 5'0" tall, so how unrealistic is that? OK, so there are many other differences too, but since this is my book, I won't go into all of those, thank you very much.)

I recently learned sometimes during a model's photo shoot, approximately 800 photos are taken and the makeup and hair styling often takes 6 hours! Surely after having someone work on my makeup and hair for that long and a professional photographer shoot 800 photos of me, a couple of good ones would come about!

Wouldn't it be cool if society saw us mothers (with a little extra pooch on our stomach because we have carried a baby or babies and it got stretched out as it was growing a life inside) and marveled at that? But instead, as soon as we have given birth, we are upset if we can't fit into our jeans immediately. Oh to instead marvel at how God has made us. He is amazing. He knit us together in our mother's wombs and He made those wombs and all the parts of the body that sustained that tiny life until it was time to be born. If I could do it all over again, I would have enjoyed my pregnancies more. Instead I just felt "fat" and since I am short (as previously mentioned) I waddled like a duck in my eighth month. I remember my husband's uncle saying, "You are so cute and radiant." It was just hard to believe. In my mind I looked like Daisy Duck in Donald's sailor suit. (Back then maternity clothes either had a big bow sewed to it somewhere where you didn't want someone's attention drawn, or a sailor collar. Go figure.) But as I look back, I wish I would have basked in that compliment.

Friday, June 30, 2006

I am getting ready to go on a vacation that includes a trip to Daytona Beach, and Katie and Nickie are appalled at a pair of tennis shoes I bought recently for the trip. They (and a couple of their friends) have made so much fun of them that I took them back (I have not worn them). If I ever wore them, I'd never hear the end of it. Nickie said if I was 75, AND blind, possibly they'd be OK. Thanks for that! My point here is that as I am putting outfits together to wear, I have been really focused on how I will look (I am single and who knows if I'll meet Mr. Right). This morning I realized I really need to be focusing on what is going on in my heart and mind and soul, more so than on my outward appearance. If I am in God's word and spending time with Him, and learning to be more like Him, the beauty that comes from Him will shine through me. This has been a prayer of mine for some time – that I would exude Christ. So if there is a Mr. Right for me, I hope he can look past the outward flaws (which are especially noticeable in a swimsuit) and see

Christ in me. Proverbs 31:30 says, *"Charm is deceptive, and beauty is fleeting, but a woman who fears the Lord is to be praised."*

Monday, July 3, 2006

This morning I picked up a book by Sheila Walsh called, *Life is Tough but God is Faithful.*[31] In it she brings up a really good point. She told the story of a young man and how when he thought of the verse, "Perfect love cast out fear," he realized he had turned it around and was living like "fear casts out perfect love." Wow. He was afraid to love due to his fear of rejection, of not being good enough. I thought about that for a while and how as a single-again woman this is true for me. After I have trusted my heart to someone (twice) and they both walked away from me, hurting me deeply, am I afraid to love again? Do I even think it is possible?

Just the other night after Katie's graduation, I took my girls and a friend of theirs out to dinner to celebrate. After we had been there for a little while, the girls noticed an attractive man sitting alone in a booth near us. Now my back was to him so they were telling me, "After God made him, He broke the mold!" I have to admit that this got my attention, but what do you really do in a situation like that? Do you just go up to a perfect (and I do mean perfect) stranger and introduce yourself? Obviously since I am asking the question, I did not do so. In fact I did absolutely nothing and that is OK. I really am not quite ready yet. Plus I believe right now God wants me to spend any spare time working on this book, and if I was dating someone, I'm pretty sure I'd be spending a lot of my spare time with him. That is not a bad thing in itself; it just isn't what I feel God wants of me right now, and I am OK with that. In fact, I am more than OK with that because I know God is working behind the scenes on my future, and I know that it will be better than anything I can even imagine (and I have quite an imagination).

Hero

Yesterday Nickie was showing me something on her "myspace" page. As she was scrolling to it, I saw listed under her "Heros" was me! I was listed third, after Jesus and her friend, Amanda, but I was also listed before Spiderman, so there! It literally brought tears to my eyes. It was confirmation I have done something right in my mothering years. It also inspires me to keep it up!

I say this because we are so often discouraged as single mothers that our kids won't turn out OK without their father in the home. I totally believe the best environment for children is to be raised in a loving home by both parents. However, when that doesn't happen, please don't lose hope. God is so good – He is the Father to the fatherless and the Husband to the husband-less. When we put our faith and trust in Him and seek Him with all our heart, He blesses us and our children. They are His children, too, and He wants them to know Him and rely on Him even more than we do.

Even though the path I have been on was not my intention for my daughters (and I sometimes feel guilty and so ashamed about our reality), as I too had the dream of living happily-ever-after while married and living in a house with a white picket fence (and a horse), but God has blessed us and sustained us even though my dreams were shattered. I believe my faith and my daughters' faith is even stronger because of the first-hand grace He has bestowed on us during our trials. Please don't hear me rejoicing in my divorce(s) as nothing could be further from the truth! But do hear me say God has been so evident to us. **I am the woman I am today because of the trials I have been through, because I have allowed God to heal me and mold me into whomever He wants me to be**. He really does know best. There is no other explanation for the hope I have, the peace in my soul, for the favor I have received, or for the excitement I feel about my future. I encourage you to do the right things, stay in God's word, be encouraged by strong Christian friends, fill your mind with positive messages and images, and God will do the rest. He is able to do more than we can even begin to imagine – so let that faith take root in your soul, water it daily with His word, and watch Him grow you into a beautiful child of God and a radiant Bride of Christ.

Saturday, July 9, 2006

I'm sitting by myself in Chicago's Midway Airport after attending the Women of Faith event here this weekend with my good friend, Lenisa. She is heading home, while I am headed to Florida for a youth event called Student Live at the Beach. The conference was wonderful as always. During the pre-conference on Friday morning, Patsy Clairmont said, "God is your credentials." Wow – I love this! I think often of writing my book, but in the back of my mind is the thought "I'm just a no-name." What I need to keep in the forefront of my mind is "I am a child of The King. He knows my name. He knows my desire to help others going through separation/divorce, to tell them of His hope and peace that surpasses understanding. Also, He is the God of the impossible – so if He has put this desire in my heart, He will see it through to completion." At the conference, Nicole C. Mullens talked about how God used people in the Bible such as Rahab and Joseph to do great things for Him. Sheila Walsh challenged us to search ourselves to see if "we really get it" – that we are loved by God.

Please keep me safe as I travel by myself (I've never done this before) and please have Your hand on the youth conference I'm heading to – that every word spoken, song sung, lesson taught and fellowship be as you would want. Help me to exude You as I interact with the students.

Saturday, July 22, 2006

I've been home from the conferences for several days and they were wonderful. In my estimation, about 1,500 teens made decisions for Christ at Student Life at the Beach. I believe approximately 7,000 teens were at the conference. Three from our youth group did so and were baptized when they returned home. What a blessing to get to be a part of this week.

Lord, right now I'd like to pray for each teen who made a decision for You. I do not know all of their names, but You do. I realize Satan will be right there telling them his lies about them not being good enough. I pray for your strength and power in their lives. Please be with them and help them overcome any temptation he will throw at them. Help them to be incredible witnesses for You. Help them go out into the world and be a light for You, as Louie Giglio challenged them. I believe You have an incredible plan for this young generation, and I am excited about that. Help us, their youth leaders, ministers and parents, to guide them and help us to truly exude You in all we do.

Ten Year Anniversary

During this Student Life Conference, what would have been my 10-year wedding anniversary came, and it hit me hard. While the students were doing their quiet time that morning, I found a spot in the corner (behind the door) and wept as I remembered our wedding, our vows, and how excited we were. Again, I was grieving the loss of my dream. But God is so faithful, because while this was going on, another youth sponsor on the trip, my friend, Cindy, decided to replenish the kitchen of the suite I was in with sugar. When she opened the door, she saw me sobbing and immediately sat down by me and spoke words of wisdom and comfort, and let me cry on her shoulder. Here's the cool thing – she is the only other youth sponsor on the trip who has been through divorce, so she really knew exactly how I felt. *Thank you, God, for my friend, and for being so personal. You knew my pain and sent a comforter. You are amazing!*

July 26, 2006

Yesterday on my ride home from work, I heard Sherry Rose Shepherd speaking on the *Focus On The Family* radio show.[54] A couple of things she said stand out in my mind. She said that God allowed healing so she could share her story and give hope to others. I feel the same way. She now speaks and has written a book. The first time she was asked to speak simply came about after telling her story to a lady at a dinner one night. She shared the realization that maybe someone's life was affected by hers. I love this because I believe I have impacted my daughters, my friends, and some of the youth group students. *Lord, help me to know Your will each day as I continue to walk with You and stay in Your word; and to truly remember that You are not going to show me Your whole plan now. That is where faith comes in – to not be able to see the physical but to know with my whole heart, mind and soul that You are presently working behind the scenes on my behalf, putting all the pieces in place for my future. Your word says, "Let it be done in accordance with your faith". Lord, I have no doubt You can do all things. Praise You! Help me never lose the wonder and awe of You and Your power!*

Monday, July 31, 2006

I have been in a funk the last several days thinking about Nickie leaving for college in a few weeks. I want to enjoy these last few weeks with her and not focus on the emptiness I'll feel when she's gone. *So, Lord, help me to do this.*

Help me to enjoy life and not just get through each day, but to really thrive and realize each day is a gift from You. I do not want to waste a single day being sad or downcast. Isn't this exactly what Satan wants? He wants me to get so focused on a tough situation I forget to focus on God! I need to remember I will not let anything steal my joy.

Tonight I read Romans 5, which talks about being thankful for trials. They produce perseverance, which produces "hope," and I thought that was pretty cool.

Tuesday, August 8, 2006

Today on my way to work, I prayed for God's favor, and then mid-morning I received an email from Louie Giglio, the author! You see, after the Student Life at the Beach conference, I wrote a short letter to him thanking him for leading the conference. It was one of the most memorable weeks of my life. Mr. Giglio's message, entitled *Indescribable*[32] was just that. He explained the hugeness of God and the not-so-bigness of us. What made this lesson so impactful was he used actual images taken by the Hubble telescope, which illustrated the size of the earth in comparison with the galaxy, and it is like a vapor. So we, therefore, are like vapor-ettes. When you consider that, it is even more remarkable how God, the Creator of the Universe, sees little ol' us! But He does, and we are precious to Him. Amazing! I would highly recommend seeing this DVD.

For me to receive a response from this well-known author and speaker was a great treat (and favor from God). Mr. Gigleo thanked me for my letter and said it was a huge encouragement to him. Wow! Sometimes I picture the "famous" speakers and singers as a little above human, and I can't imagine them really needing encouragement (because I'm sure they are perfect and have it all together), especially from a no name like me. Thankfully, we are all God's children, and maybe in this instant God used me, the "weak," to encourage Mr. Giglio, the "strong." God just continues to amaze me.

Saturday, August 12, 2006

Today I woke up and pretty much immediately cried. In less than two weeks I will take "my baby" to college and LEAVE her there! Oh, how I will sorely miss her at home every day. She is such a joy (most of the time) and I will miss her smile, laughter and antics each day. I am dreading it! There is a real, tangible pain in my heart. How have so many mothers dealt with this? What will it be like each day to come home and know she won't be here? I think the pain I feel is grief – grieving the fact that nothing as I know it will be the same. Soon Katie will be out on her own, too. Within a two-year period, it feels as though I've lost my family.

I never dreamed I'd be alone at this stage in my life, and that makes me even more aware of the blessing of having Gina here. What I thought would be a blessing for her has really become a blessing for me, so thank You, Lord, for working that all out. I do not fear being alone, my incredible friends and family keep me from feeling lonely. I know I am truly never alone – my God is always with me! Thank You, God!

Maybe there is some fear of the unknown. What does my future hold? Will I find God's plan or purpose for me?

Lord, please give me Your peace each day and don't allow me to wallow in self-pity or become depressed, but to be courageous when I need to call a friend. Often it is hard to make the call but a real friend (and I am blessed with many) would be open to hear from me when I'm hurting, so I need to not let my pride get in the way.

God, do you ever cry? I mean if we are "made in your likeness," then I believe you probably do. I am certain we grieve You sometimes. Just as I hurt letting Katie and Nickie go (which is a good and maturing process) You must like-wise hurt when one of us strays, and especially when one who was close to You walks away. How it must pain You to see us hurt each other or to deny You after all You have done for us.

Yesterday it rained really hard and I couldn't help but think of the rain as Your tears. You must be grieved at all the sin and hate in the world. I was listening to the song called "Reign Down" by Delirious[34] *during this downpour. In Noah's day, You literally used the rain to cleanse the earth. In these days, when we sing this song I think we are asking You to reign over the earth – to have things Your way in each of us. That's a pretty good prayer.*

Please Lord, reign in me – give me Your patience, Your peace, Your wisdom, Your grace and Your favor. I still want to get to know You so well that Your word is on my heart and in my mind so that people will see You in me. I already feel better after this writing, so thank You.

Sunday, Aug. 13, 2006

This morning as I was getting ready for church, I had the radio tuned in to a show called *The Heart of Worship.*[55] I love listening to this before church because it plays different worship songs from all over the country, and sometimes there is a brief interview with a worship leader or songwriter. This morning they played the song, "He Knows My Name," [35] and the songwriter told the beautiful story behind the song. It's about how we all want someone to know our name and how marvelous it is that God, the Creator does! Then, we sang this same song at church today! We hardly ever sing this song. So is this God telling me I'm exactly where I am supposed to be? I just love it when that happens!

August 16, 2006

Today as I was driving to work, I was singing along with the song on our local Christian radio station, and this lady cut me off on the expressway. She zoomed up behind me and cut over next to me, leaving me no place to go as I was merging onto the highway! Hello, why do people do that? The merge lane is only so long! Anyway, I noticed I went from singing praises to God to immediately saying something like, "What are you, an idiot? Did you get your drivers license from Sears?" After I skillfully maneuvered my car onto the highway, I remembered the following verse in James 3:9 "*With the tongue we praise our Lord and Father, and with it we curse men, who have been made in God's likeness. Out of the same mouth comes praise and cursing.*" Guilty. So I said a quick prayer for the lady driver in her white Acura; that she'd get where she was going safely, 'cause she was driving f-a-s-t.

Saturday, August 26, 2006

Wow, what a week! Actually, wow, what a couple of weeks! We've been busy getting Nickie ready to go away to college. This continues to be a grieving process for me. I cry at the drop of a hat. I was helping her pack up her clothing, and when I went back into her closet and saw it almost empty, I just started sobbing uncontrollably. Not only do I imagine what it will be like when I came home each day from work and she won't be here, but she is my youngest child, so it is making me face my identity apart from being a mother, my main role for the last 19 years of my life.

Thankfully I am not alone in this, as there are about five other women at church going through the same experience and feelings. We've been teasing about starting a support group at church and calling it the WACKOS (Wailing Adults of College Kids Offering Support). (My friend, LuAnn came up with that. She is so clever.) Trust me, this name applies to us in more ways than one! The funny thing is our kids are doing great! I think a couple may be a little homesick, but overall they are having a great time away from us. So we aren't really crying about them, we are truly crying for ourselves – yep, it is all about us! We miss them and are wondering what in the world we are supposed to do now that our kids are raised. I think I am the only single one, so I explained to one of the ladies today this is the time for her and her husband to do things together. Since I am single, I can daydream about having a spouse and all the things we could do together and places we could go. (I have quite the imagination, and in my daydreams, an endless budget.) But it seems reality is not so glamorous. One lady told me today she just feels like her own entity in her own home. It seems the fathers/husbands aren't grieving and really don't understand what the women are going through. One woman doesn't even cry in front of her husband.

Lord, I lift these ladies up to you. Please comfort them as only You can and lead them to know what their purpose is. Remind them You still have a plan for them; they aren't done since their children are raised. Help us to encourage and love each other.

After crying the whole drive to college, finding her dorm and setting it up (it looks so cute), I was fine. We drove to a Wal-Mart (now I'm assured she is fine, as she can get anything she needs there) and to Southland Christian Church in Lexington so she would know where to go to meet a friend who is attending UK on the Sundays they don't come home. (How proud am I that she has already pondered and set this up?) However, during this entire drive, she cried, so she still has absolutely no idea how to get to Southland, but it was good she had this time to get these tears out of her system. She was nervous, and I totally understand. She is almost 18, moving to a new town, into a new room, with a new room-mate, and a new church, and without her mom's home cooking. (OK, so she didn't openly admit to the last one, but I'm sure it was on her mind. Ha Ha.)

When we arrived back on campus (we skipped the "parent meeting" and the "welcoming ceremony" as rumor has it that they just make the parents cry, and I needed no help with that. You'd think they were getting paid for our tears!), it was about time for her to attend her first orientation event, so we hugged each other tightly, and I will admit that we both shed some more tears. Then she got out of the car and headed back to her dorm to get ready. She called me the next day and was doing great. She's made some new friends already (I knew she would. She is a doll and has a great personality – must get it from her momma).

When I talked to my counselor last week about my grieving, she reassured me when we love, we get attached, and that is the reason for the grief. She reminded me it is better to love and grieve than not to have loved at all.

Sunday, August 27, 2006

Today at church, we hosted a Missionary Fair. About twenty missionaries from organizations our church supports attended. At the end of the service, these missionaries went up on the platform and we prayed for them. I noticed that one of them was really cute. He was tall, dark and handsome, so I asked my friend, who is the church secretary, if she knew who he was (after the service, of course). While at the Missionary Fair, I saw he was married and had children. So after some time visiting with people at the fair, I came home to a voice mail message from my friend. Her message said, "There are two problems. He lives in Ecuador, which is too far away for you to be from me, and he is married with kids." I just started laughing out loud. It just struck me as so funny that the *first* problem was he lives too far away! What a great friend she is to check into this for me; and to be sure I don't get too far away from her. Her husband said he didn't think he was up to my caliber! Hello . . . the man is a missionary, so I hardly think that could be correct, but how touching that even he seems to be looking out for my best interests. I love them!

During the sermon, one of our mission committee members was talking about a mission trip he was on, I think in Indonesia, and one of the men there said to him in his own language he must be an ambassador of God as he had been instrumental in getting electric run to this village. This struck me because just last night during my quiet time I read 2 Corinthians 5:6 -21 and in verse 20, it says, "*We are therefore Christ's ambassadors . . .*" Wow, I just love when this happens. Again, I feel it is God reminding me I am exactly where I am supposed to be. How amazing that God, the Creator, cares enough about me, one little woman in Kentucky.

Also in church today, I thought about how I have no right to ask Jesus for anything. He was in heaven, being praised by the angels, on a throne amongst beauty we can't even fathom, but because He and the Father love us so much, He left all that glory and splendor voluntarily to come to earth. He was born amongst the stench of a barnyard; He became flesh so He could communicate with us about God's incredible love. He felt pain. He cried. And his sole purpose was to die the cruelest death imaginable after being here for 33 years. I cannot imagine knowing my ultimate purpose would be to be crucified. Of course, He knew He would be raised by His Father, but still I wonder if ever He thought, "These people don't deserve this sacrifice." And He'd be right. But isn't my ultimate purpose also to die, to die to myself and my selfish desires, and instead to focus on Him, His truths and His desires for my life: His ultimate purpose for me? **So His purpose and my purpose will**

then become the same. But God is amazing, because as I have no rights to ask for anything, He tells us we are free to do so. In James 4:2, it says, "*We do not have because we do not ask.*" He is our loving Father and He longs to give us "gifts." Amazing.

Thursday, September 7, 2006

Tonight I went to a divorce recovery support group with Angie. This time, because Angie was with me, I was able to walk into the room, but if she would not have been, I probably would have pretended I was looking for another class and just passed it up and left. Even though I have been doing pretty well lately, for some reason this class almost brought tears to my eyes. There was just something about being there . . . it was like a public admission that, yep, I'm one of the statistics – a loser, rejected. The facilitator said the class would probably bring up some painful feelings but to come back, as that is part of the healing process. How long does this healing take? Listening to the others in the room, it appears most of these people are newly divorced or separated, so at least I can see that I am "ahead of the class" (a first for me, I can assure you). The facilitator also told us there is a more structured workshop class (complete with a workbook) that meets on Monday nights. I'm thinking since I may want to help others through this painful life experience, I should go to that one. The first one is next Monday. Angie has a class at school that night, so I may have to gather up my courage and go by myself. Yikes!

Sunday, September 10, 2006

Last weekend Katie, Nickie, Gina and I were in New York City with LuAnn and her daughter, Amanda; we had a fabulous time. When it was time for Nickie to leave on Tuesday to go back to school, I cried. I mean, I'd just gotten used to having her with me for four whole days. I told her if there wasn't a need for her to come home this weekend that she should stay at school because it just kills me when it is time for her to leave again. I know this is probably very normal, but I feel like such a baby.

Yesterday I was reading a *Today's Christian Woman*[36] magazine and came across a quote from Patricia Raybon from her book entitled, *Mountain Mover.* It said, "Prayer is less talking, more listening to God; less asking, more dwelling with God, enjoying His amazing presence." Wow! I got to thinking, do I really know how to pray? I pray a lot throughout the day, but most of the time I am either thanking Him or asking for something. This isn't bad, as He said we do not have because we do not ask, and I usually don't ask for material blessings or even for selfish things. But I do all of the talking. If I was having a conversation with one of my girlfriends and I did all the talking, I imagine they would get pretty put out, roll their eyes, try to get a word in, and eventually leave since I am not allowing them to respond. But when I am quiet in prayer, my mind wanders, or if I have a thought I question if it is from God or just from my vivid imagination.

So, Lord, I need Your help here. Show me how to just be still and dwell with You. Please help me to hear from You and to know it is from You.

Today, my minister, Rick, explained "our crosses" are not circumstances that are dealt us such as blindness or cancer, but instead are tough circumstances to teach us **patient endurance** to mold us to be like Christ. Wow! It was perfect timing for me to hear this. Just a couple of weeks ago, I was talking with my mom about my book and explained I have no idea when I'll be finished with it. I don't know how or when to end it and she said, "You'll end it when you have had some victories; you know in a couple of years or so." My immediate response was, "What, a couple of years?! Hello, there are people out there who are hurting, and I want to help now." As you can see, I failed the patient endurance part of the test. I want to wrap this up and get on with the process of looking for an editor or whatever else I am supposed to do, but maybe she is right (I've learned she usually is). Maybe God wants me to experience the victory of totally healing from the divorce. Maybe He wants me to have more to share about the final years of raising my girls as a single mom, and the trials and victories that will come from that. Maybe He even wants me to meet the man of my dreams and explain our dating relationship, and the rewards of doing it all God's way (OK, so I am a certified dreamer). So today I was convinced I need to work on my patience with this process and not get ahead of God, because I definitely know if this book even comes to be, it will be all from Him and for Him.

Lord, help me to work on my praying, too, to concentrate on being still and listening for You. I truly cannot imagine anything more powerful than the feeling of being in Your presence, so help me to remember that each day. Help me to not get discouraged or succumb to loneliness. Help me, too, to know what You want me to do with my life. Help me to never forget that even when I can't see it, You are working behind the scenes putting things in place for my perfect plan.

XI

Divorce Recovery

Sunday, September 17, 2006

On Monday I went to a DivorceCare[2] Workshop at Southeast Christian Church. I was not particularly looking forward to it. In fact my counselor made me promise to attend at least three classes, and I know she is right. This time, unlike a year ago, I got up the courage and **actually walked into the room**. Last time, I did a 360 and almost ran out of the place when a man entered the room! This time I was surprised when a friend of mine was in there. I absolutely hate she is going through this trial, but if she has to, how good of God to allow us to go through it together. He is amazing! After being welcomed to the class, we watched a DVD about divorce. I was encouraged by it because it seems I am on the healing path. The "experts" in the video explained the pain of divorce is so deep because two lives have been joined and then ripped apart. They further explained the only way to truly heal is *to go through* *the pain.* Sometimes it is so painful people want to cover that pain with alcohol or drugs or a new relationship, but that only leads to deeper unresolved pain that will eventually come to the surface. They stressed the importance of getting counseling, drawing closer to God, and having same-sex friends. Yes!!! I've been doing all three, and I feel good about those decisions.

Yesterday I attended a session for women leaders at a local church. I am not currently serving in this role, but I can't help but feel that maybe some day I will be called to because the desire of my heart is to bring hope to hurting women who have been devastated by divorce. The speaker was a nice lady who said she really wasn't a speaker; she left that to her husband who was the president of a Christian college, but was asked to do this, so she acquiesced. She did a really nice job of explaining that, as Christian women, we are to spend quiet time with God each day and find out how we can be effective for His kingdom. She explained after God, our next priority is our husbands. (I know this is counter-cultural, and we hate to hear this and realize the dreaded "submissive" word is going to soon come up, and then we think, puhlease . . . they are grown men for heavens sake and I have children to take care of!) But she is correct, as much as I hate to admit it. We are to care for our husbands and put their needs before ours. I think God's plan is when we do that, they are more than willing to treat us with respect and even to die for us. But in every day life, this is so difficult, and I think Satan knows that and he gets us every time. I took this to heart and came home wondering, "Lord, did I not do this correctly?" I really tried to put my husband first most of the time, but on some days when my children had a school event or were sick, they had to take priority.

Isn't that OK? Aren't we called to be great mothers, too? Shouldn't a grown man understand that?

She told a story of a young lady who had become pregnant out of wedlock. She and her husband have helped raise the child and sometimes, even today, she gets frustrated with her because she makes some bad choices. Then she said, "I understand since she came from a home where her mom was married two times and her father was married three times she really didn't have any role models." Ouch! I felt like I had been punched in the stomach. At first I was a little hurt and I think my face may have turned a light shade of red, because that is me! . . . not by my choice, but I'm the mom who has been married twice. I think, though, I have still been a role model to my daughters, even a good one (most of the time). I have taught them about unconditional love, about how to go on even when you don't have the strength, about the importance of working hard (even if it takes two jobs) to pay for things that are important, and many other lessons that come from tough times. But most importantly, I have taught them about Christ since they were infants, and they have witnessed His numerous blessings and unexplainable provisions through both of my divorces and my journeys as a single mom.

I am not mad at this lady, as she is a wonderful wife and mother who keeps her home clean and orderly and practices the gift of hospitality by taking food to hurting families in church, and who truly wants to encourage other women to be witnesses for Christ. But, I learned an important lesson for myself. I need to be careful with my words, especially if I ever get to speak to a group of people. She obviously had no intention of hurting anyone, and this was a good thing for me to feel so I can remember to never generalize.

Tuesday, September 26, 2006

Last night I went to my third DivorceCare[2] class. The topic was anger. I was again encouraged because I believe I have come a long way.

Today I received an interesting email called, "*Worklife Lessons: A Leader Like That.*" In it the author talks about Jesus picking the apostles and how "He always focused not on the failures of the moment among his tiny band of workers, but rather on that moment in the future when the mission finally made it from the pages of scripture to their heads and hearts." I love the fact Jesus didn't and still does not focus on our "failures of the moment." What hope I have that instead He is pulling for me and waiting for me to totally believe in Him and let His word live in and through me and shine out to others. Also, what an incredible example of how we should be with others. When we can look past someone's failures, we are extending grace, and what a great way to be Christ-like.

I've thought about grace with one of my daughter's bad decisions. I had a "come to Jesus" meeting and set some strict rules to reel her in for a time. But what an opportunity for me to be a living example of Christ for her – to show her I still love her and I know she has an incredible future ahead of her. I haven't let this one "failure of the moment" define who she is, and I don't want her to either.

I've been thinking about dating. Not that I've had any offers, which is probably good because I want to be sure no matter what happens, or who would ask me out someday, I want to be able to have God as my ultimate relationship. I truly want Him to be the love of my life.

I love when I fall asleep, wake up in the middle of the night, or wake up in the morning, my thoughts are almost always on God, either with a prayer or a scripture verse or words from a song on my lips. I believe this comes from saturating my mind with His word. I pretty much only listen to contemporary Christian music because I love the messages in the songs. I *need* to continually hear the positive messages in the songs especially at this time in my life while I am healing.

I try to have quiet time almost every night. I love it and look forward it. It is more than just reading some words from the Bible; it is about inviting God, the Creator of All, into my time and asking Him to speak to me, even though I am so unworthy of His time and attention. But I am his child, and He loves me more than I can even imagine. What an honor!

So, back to the subject of dating. Maybe I would put a guy before God now, so if that is the case, Lord, then help me to be content and joy-filled in my singleness. I have an excitement about my future even though I do not know what You plan for me, but I know You have good plans for me and I thank You in advance for that.

Today the verse, "*You do not have because you do not ask*" (James 4:2) came into my mind as I was driving to work. *So, Lord I'm asking You, with total faith You can do anything, that my book will be what You want it to be. That You will lead me or bring people into my life to assist with the editing and publishing, and it would get into the peoples' hands who need to hear about Your power and love and healing in my life so they can truly know You desire to do the same for them. Help me find an organization to help so the proceeds can go to them and help them in a tangible way first, and then maybe they'd be open to hearing the Gospel message. Lord, I know I am a no-name by the world's standards, but You not only know my name, You know my heart. If You choose to use me in this way, it would be an honor and a privilege. I want to give all the credit to You.*

This brings back memories from Women of Faith where Patsy Clairmont said, "God is your credentials." Wow – I just love that! I can't think of any credentials I'd rather have.

A couple of weeks ago, the president of a Christian college spoke at church about leadership. He said we don't have the skills and/or resources to do something, but God purposefully chooses people who think they are incapable so they won't boast. Jesus demonstrated this idea when He chose unlearned men to be his apostles, and they have left quite a legacy!

It just feels as though the desire for this book comes from You – it is so deep in my heart. Help me to know Your plan and help me follow You each day. It is a big world and I can't imagine all You'll do. I am Yours – a broken vessel, but You have put the pieces back together and are making me a new creation. I pray Your light will shine through my brokenness. Lord, again today, I pray to let me exude You – I want Your eyes Father, so when people look into my eyes, they'll see You and Your amazing grace, love, acceptance, peace, kindness, forgiveness and compassion.

Tuesday, October 3, 2006

It is a warm night for October in Kentucky, and I feel a nice breeze blowing through my windows – how refreshing. I love the days and nights like this when I can have my windows open and listen to the crickets. It reminds me of summer days and nights I spent at my grandma's house in the country when I was a child. I have some wonderful memories of her and those times. My grandma was a true servant. What a role model. She couldn't wait for us to come from the city to see her. She'd cook a wonderful meal and would hardly even eat any herself because she wanted to wait on every one of us. It was truly the joy of her life to have her whole family together around her table. I think she smiled the whole time we were there. I can't help but think about how much like God that is. I believe that, like my grandma, He desires to have all His children around His grand table some day. I know I can't wait, and I hope to sit by my grandma, so I can finally watch her eat.

Yesterday one of my bosses surprised me with a "personal" question, which is rare for him to ask. (He's an engineer. Enough said.) He said, "Should we be praying for a husband for you?" I was so shocked I about fell out of my chair as I laughed nervously. I told him I'm not quite ready for that. I went on to explain I really am enjoying this time of singleness now. I have time to write and I so look forward to my quiet time. If I was dating right now, that would take up some of this time and energy. But I also said when I'm ready, I'd be sure to let him and his wife know, as they are some mighty prayer warriors and I truly respect them. (His wife has warned me to not let him fix me up with anyone. She says she's lost a couple of good friends that way!)

Since he brought up this subject, I have to admit the idea of going out does appeal to me a little. It has been almost two years since Brady left, and I have worked very hard on healing. With God's help I am on the right track. I don't know if anyone ever totally heals from a devastating life event like the death of a loved one or a divorce, but hopefully we can learn through the pain and carry those lessons with us throughout our lives and help others who will also walk in those shoes. I was reminded last night that God does not waste a hurt. If we will allow, He can mold us into better people, more like God even, and use our experiences to help another one of His children. In fact, I think that may be the definition of ministry.

Necessary Depression

One of my DivorceCare[2] classes focused on depression, and I learned healing cannot occur without depression. Wow. I hated to hear this because I believed I had avoided this during my situation. It was explained that there are different levels of depression. Depression can include feeling sad and unworthy and not caring about anything. It often drains your energy and makes you feel like isolating yourself. Some days just getting out of bed is an accomplishment. If we don't get somewhat depressed, we're not dealing with the loss.

Some do, unfortunately, get so depressed they may become suicidal. If that is you, please call someone and get help immediately. God has created you and He loves you and He has an amazing plan for your life – one that is even too good to imagine, so please seek help immediately.

No one wants to go through pain, but the only way to truly heal is to go through it – not around it. Some people will try to anesthetize the pain with drugs, alcohol, food or even another relationship, according to the DivorceCare[2] professionals. But this does about as much good as putting a band-aid on a cut that needs stitches. It may be a temporary fix, but sooner or later you will have to deal with the pain.

Saturday, October 7, 2006

Friday I came home from work and in my mailbox was one of the most beautiful cards I'd ever received. It was from my ex's father. (I also received Chris Tomlin's new CD, complete with an autographed cover, so I was smiling as I entered my front door). The card was homemade on his computer, and the front cover simply had one word on it: "Daughter," along with a bear hugging a bunny on a sunny day. On the inside was the most tender note, and it made me cry. It said how he misses me, and how grateful he is to have had me as a part of his life, if only for a season, and I was welcome at his home anytime. He is proud of me and praying for God's blessings on me. Now we aren't talking about some wimpy man. He was a truck driver by trade. He seems to have a soft place in his heart for me. What a blessing. He doesn't even know all that has happened, to my knowledge, and does not understand why there was a divorce. He still loves his son with his whole heart, as he should, but how wonderful he was so vulnerable and shared his feelings with me.

As I write this, I can't help but think how this is so much like our Father God – He has a soft spot in his heart for each of us, and no matter what we have done or how far away from Him we have gone, we are welcome to come to Him anytime!

Have you ever listened to a song and all of a sudden feel so touched that tears start to fall from your eyes? Today I listed to Chris Tomlin's version of "Amazing Grace"[37] for the first time, and it is a beautiful arrangement. He has added a bridge (I believe that is the technical music term for it) that includes the lyrics, "My chains are gone. I've been set free . . . un-ending love. Amazing Grace." It brought to mind how thankful I am God has cut the chains to my past, mistakes, and sins. I am a new creation, and by God's grace I have a future – an amazing and abundant future.

Lord, my heart is full of joy, excitement and expectation! Thank You! I know You only have good things in store for me. Please, fill me daily and help me to never lose the awe and wonder of You.

Sunday, October 8, 2006

Tonight after Bible Study I fixed one of our toilets, on my own, with my bare hands. I am woman, hear me roar! I just didn't feel like dishing out $100 for a plumber, so I simply flushed the one in my bathroom a couple of times to see how it worked and compared that to the one that was not working. I discovered the problem and fixed it. Now my hands are blue from the Tidy Bowl® cleaner. I came running down the hall and yelled, "I am so good!" Then it hit me that the blue was not coming off as I washed my hands! What will I do if I actually get to meet Chris Tomlin Thursday at his concert and shake his hand and he says, "Very nice to meet you . . . really, the pleasure is all mine . . . why are your hands blue?" (I am such a dreamer.) What do I say? I guess I'd have to be truthful and hope he'd be impressed with a woman who can fix her own toilet (with her bare hands no less) as well as know quality music when she hears it! Ha.

I am counting this as a victory. My mom said I may need a couple more before this book is ready, so I'm hoping this one counts. I'm getting anxious to get this edited, published and whatever else it takes. But, Lord, I know Your timing is perfect so please keep guiding me and let me know when You are finished writing this through me.

Monday, October 9, 2006

Tonight I went to my fourth DivorceCare[2] class, and the subject was loneliness. The "experts" went quite deep with this topic. Basically they explained that the word "single" means 1) separate, 2) unique, 3) whole. They explained most people who get married are looking for these qualities – they are looking to be single. How wild is that? We just can't be pleased, can we?

They further explained that often times people who have been divorced get into rebound relationships quickly just to keep from being lonely. This often leads to a quick marriage, which is not conducive to a stable foundation. Most times, this marriage will fail too. (Yep, that's mine. I did not spend time healing between my marriages, and my second husband did not either.) Also, it is healthy to spend time alone. We need to be able to heal, and to really see who we are and who we want to become and to spend time with God to find out what His plan is for us. I was listening to a song with the lyrics "Is this who you want to be . . . is life all you dreamed?"[38] It encourages the listener to look at his/her life and make changes if you are not happy with it.

Pick-Up Lines?

Here's a funny story that happened at class last night. I'll call it *Pick-Up Lines 101*. During our five-minute break between the DVD and our small group time, a guy in the class came up to me and said, "So are you 4'9" tall?" (In my head, I thought, "Look buddy, if that is a pick-up line, you need to get another one. I mean, hello, when someone is short, every tenth of an inch is important to them so you need to say something like, "Hey are you about 5'3" tall" and watch them stand a little taller.) But instead I kindly said as I stood to my full height, "Actually I am 5 foot tall, thank you very much." And then he said, "Well good things come in small packages." Yikes. So I just said, "Yes they do." Then I quickly scurried out of the room and into the comfort of my small group. (Seems to me he really needed to listen during the loneliness class.) I don't know if I have a lesson for you here, but I just thought it was a funny story I'd share. Oh, but this brings to mind another funny story about a bad pick-up line.

Years ago, before my second marriage, a group of my friends and I went to a "singles Christmas party" that one of the guys in our church was hosting at his house. This was probably the first singles outing my friend, Mary, and I had attended. We were both nervous and not really sure we wanted any part of it. We went because of our friends' coaxing. Pretty soon after we arrived, one of the single guys spied my friend Mary (who is a doll, by the way). He approached and asked her name and about her job. She politely told him that she worked at one of the local hospitals to which he replied he had been there before – when he had to have hemorrhoids removed. Hello! Way too much information! I could not help but laugh hysterically, and I'm pretty sure Coke may have spewed from my nose as I laughed hysterically! I quickly exited the room with Mary close behind. Needless to say, we didn't stay too long, and I don't think we ever went to another "singles Christmas party." Oh, but what a memory! I don't know how many times we have laughed about it!

Tuesday, October 10, 2006 2:00 AM

I don't know why I can't sleep except I think I am excited about my future. Remember when you where a kid and you were going to leave the next day for Disney World and you couldn't sleep the night before? I'm not going anywhere later today except to work, but I have this excitement in my heart about God's plans for my life. My counselor told me she is proud of me. Now that I have done a lot of hard work on healing, excitement and fun is just around the corner. I am so ready! The possibilities are endless with God. Hopefully this book will come to fruition and will help many to see His amazing love and restoration power. Maybe I'll actually get to speak to groups of women, or maybe I'll get to travel and help on the mission field. Maybe God actually does have a loving, authentic Christian man for me some day to serve with. Whatever He has planned, I know it will be better than anything I can even imagine. I want to be sure I stay in the center of His will. I want to be sure I don't try to figure it all out on my own because without God, it is destined to fail.

This has gotten me to thinking of some of the incredible people in our culture who have impacted the world for God; people such as Reverend Billy Graham, Mother Theresa, Max Lucado, Bob Russell, Beth Moore, Steven Curtis Chapman, Louie Giglco and Chris Tomlin, just to name a few. And I wonder, why them? I'm thinking it is because of their evident love for God and their total surrender to Him. I imagine at one point in their lives they simply said, "God, I am yours. Send me." And He did. They have done extraordinary things for the Kingdom – things that are bigger than they are, things that took miracles from God. So can this happen for me too? Can it happen for you? I believe if we truly believe all things are possible for God and can see it through our spiritual eyes, and stay connected to God through His word, our dreams (God's dreams) for our lives can come true. One of my favorite scriptures is Psalm 37:4, "*If I will delight in the Lord, He will give me the desires of my heart.*" I desire to be used by Him, so Lord, Here I am. Send me.

I have been reading another great book called *Pursuing Your Life Dream*[39] by Eastman Curtis. In chapter 7 he says, "God is looking for someone who will dare to dream big. He is looking for someone who is willing to believe that He can do anything. He is looking for someone who will dare to believe He has a miracle for them." I love this!

He also states, "Rarely does the provision come before the vision. That as you move toward the vision God placed in your heart, you will see the provision come." [40] He also talked about the importance of speaking about your dreams, so I'll work on this one.

Friday, October 13, 2006

Last night I went to see Chris Tomlin in concert at The Palace with Gina. We had a great time. He was so intentional on letting us know this was not a usual concert where we sit back and eat popcorn and enjoy the music, but instead it is a worship event for God – our audience of One. He went on to say they aren't the attraction, and we aren't the audience. But instead, all of us together are the performers blessing God. His heart is so full of love and adoration for God and that is the most attractive thing to me – someone so openly sold out to God. Oh, how I pray I, too, will become so bold for Christ. During the "service" as I listened to him, I couldn't help but think of the scripture, "*From the overflow of the heart the mouth speaks.*" I mentioned this to Gina after the performance on our way to find dessert before we headed home.

Today after work I decided to catch-up on the Bible study our whole church is doing, as I am one day behind due to the concert last night. So I flipped open to the lesson for October 12 (the night of the concert) and the scripture reading was Matthew 12: 15-50 which just happens to include verse 34, "*For out of the overflow of the heart, the mouth speaks?*". Hello? I laughed so hard I almost fell out of my chair. God, is this from You? Do you have a big smile on Your face at my delight? Did You give me that verse last night to let me know I am right where I am supposed to be now?

The Bible study lesson asked, "What weeds are choking out my faith and full surrender?" I think the answer is doubt and fear of failing. I don't doubt God's capability to bring about my dreams at all, but I tend to wonder if my dreams are really from Him or from me alone. So Lord, I continue to pray for your guidance. Proverbs 10:24 says, ". . . *what the righteous desire will be granted.*" Psalm 25:14 says, "*The Lord confides in those who fear Him; He makes his covenant known to them.*" And Psalms 32:8 says, "*I will instruct you and teach you in the way you should go; I will counsel you and watch over you.*" Lord, I really want to claim these promises. Please speak to me and help me to be still so I can hear.

Sunday, October 15, 2006

Today after church, my dear friend Barbara came up to me and said through tears, "Annette, God is going to use you." I was hoping maybe He had spoken to her in a dream and she was going to give me some visuals. Instead she went on to explain how just this week one of her friend's husband left her after 26 years of marriage. They were all in shock and heart-broken. She wanted my advice on what she should do for her. Then, another friend confided in me that she and her husband are having problems. She said, "I don't want to lose him." Oh, my heart is heavy this afternoon. What is going on in our culture? Why can't people love their spouses as Christ loved the church?

Lord, if I can be of any encouragement or help to these ladies, please guide me in knowing what to say. But more importantly, Lord, You are God the Healer, so I lift these two couples up to you. Please touch these men's hearts as only You can and convict them that Your desire for them is to remain in their marriages and with You all things are possible. You even desire for them to have meaningful marriages, marriages they could only dream about.

Monday, October 16, 2006

Maybe I am to be single for the rest of my life, or maybe for just a short time. Honestly, I hope the later is the plan, as I loved being married and long to have someone special to share my life with some day. *Right now I need to continue to heal and focus on writing and on whatever else You have in mind for me, so Lord, please guide me each day of my life.*

My counselor, Debbie, explained that marriage is a ministry. What a great thought . . . not one we usually consider.

I believe most of us get married thinking, "What will I get out of it" instead of "how can I serve or minister to my spouse?" We often get married because we don't want to be alone or grow old by ourselves, but marriage is really about helping and encouraging our spouse to be the best person he is meant to be. It really isn't about what we will get out of it. Debbie said she thinks God sometimes looks down at us when we pray for a spouse and says, "Girl, you've got too much on your plate for another ministry right now." And His withholding at this time is a blessing. I love that!

XII

Hard Teachings From The Bible

In my DivorceCare class, we talked about God's design for marriage. At first I thought that was sort of a silly topic since we are all coming out of one, and I didn't really look forward to getting "beat up" by the Bible and its stance on divorce. But I actually learned a lot. We've all heard the verse, "God hates divorce". And He does, but He does not hate the divorced person, no matter who the "guilty" party is. In Psalm 147:3 it says, "*God heals the brokenhearted*" and I believe both parties are truly brokenhearted. Praise Him for his unfailing love! He is the author of marriage and I believe divorce grieves Him, because He knows how many people are impacted and hurt through it. God intends marriage to be a life-long commitment, and I believe when most of us said our wedding vows, we had the same intentions.

So what went wrong? I think part of the problem is our expectations of marriage. We buy into the vision everything is going to be perfect and we'll "live happily ever after." If our spouse doesn't agree with us, we can change them. But the Bible even talks about troubles in marriage, because God knows when you put two people under one roof, there will be disagreements and differing opinions. We are all unique, and were raised differently. When you add children to that mix, there can be chaos. Even in the church, we often get so excited and caught up with the wedding, reception, and honeymoon we don't plan effectively for the marriage itself. I heard of a billboard in Texas that says, "Nice Wedding; Invite Me for the Marriage – God."

My understanding is that God allows divorce in two circumstances. This is some hard teaching because if we truly desire to do God's will, we have to really look to see if we fit into these situations. If you don't, I would encourage you to seek God and, if possible, seek reconciliation, as I believe that is the perfect plan (in most situations where there is not abuse). With God's help, and a sincere willingness to reconcile by both parties, your marriage could be better than you could ever imagine, because that is just how God is. He is the master at taking broken pieces and making something beautiful from them.

The DivorceCare[2] professionals explained the most known "acceptable" reason for divorce, according to the Bible, is adultery. In Matthew 19:7-9, the religious leaders asked Jesus, "*Why then, did Moses command that a man give his wife a certificate of divorce and send her away?" Jesus replied, "Moses permitted you to divorce your wives because your hearts were hard. But it was not that way from the beginning. I tell you that anyone who divorces his wife, except for marital unfaithfulness, and marries another woman commits adultery.*"

In our class, we talked about how adultery here probably refers to continuous adultery. If the person had a one-night stand, as hard and painful as that is to you, if he/she is repentant and wants to get help and work on the marriage, most professionals would say to do so. What an opportunity to really "walk the walk" of Christ by forgiving and extending grace.

The second circumstance in which the Bible allows divorce is the departure of an unbeliever. In I Corinthians 7:15 it says, "*But if the unbeliever leaves, let him do so. A believing man or woman is not bound in such circumstances; God has called us to live in peace.*"

Here is the hard part of the DVD, in my opinion. In these two circumstances, we have the **right** to divorce, but we also have the privilege to forgive and show grace and try to reconcile. You might be thinking that is the last thing I feel like doing. He/she has wounded me deeply and I don't want to see them again, much less think about reconciliation. That is understandable, and that is where your faith in God comes in. I would encourage you to spend some time in His word, in prayer, and He'll guide you. He really is still the God of the miraculous.

Here is some more tough teaching from the Bible. It may step on some toes. "*To the married I give this command (not I, but the Lord): A wife must not separate from her husband. But if she does, she must remain unmarried or else be reconciled to her husband. And a husband must not divorce his wife.*" I Corinthians 7:10-11. You see, divorcing because you just don't love each other anymore is not a Biblical precedent for divorce, according to the DivorceCare[2] experts. Look at that verse carefully. Notice is says, "but if she does (separate) she must remain unmarried." Why do you think that is in there? I think it is because God knows that we have a natural desire to be married, to have a life partner, to not be alone, to have someone think we are special, so after a divorce we start scoping to see who is out there to meet those needs for us. I'll confess I have thought about what it would be like to be married when I've seen a cute guy at the gym or somewhere. I've even envisioned myself being proposed to and walking down the aisle. See what I mean? I am already thinking about the wedding itself, for crying out loud! If we know we are to remain single if we are leaving a marriage where there has not been any adultery or abuse by our spouse, it may make us think harder about our decision to leave. Trading our spouse in for a newer model isn't an option according to the Bible. God is making it hard for us to get a divorce because He hates it and what it does to families.

If you are in a marriage where there is abuse, please get yourself and your children to safety immediately. You don't have to know all the answers now, just seek help and protection. I'm going out on a limb here, but I just don't see a loving God wanting you to stay in that situation unless the abusive spouse is getting help to change. Notice I said "getting help," which means taking some action on their part, not just *promising* to change. A separation doesn't necessarily mean divorce. Sometimes it lets the other party know you are serious and if they want to stay in the marriage, they have to make some much-needed changes, like getting counseling or going to a treatment center if there is alcohol or drug abuse.

OK, so ready for some more hard teaching? According to God, we are only allowed to remarry if we were the "innocent" party in the divorce, meaning we were the one abandoned and not involved in adultery. Obviously, none of us are totally innocent in our marriages because we are human and we all sin.

If you are reading this and you didn't do things biblically, I don't want you to think that God doesn't love you, because nothing could be further from the truth. God still loves you no matter what you have done. See, when Jesus shed his blood for our sin, He did so to cover all sin (yep, even divorce) and if you don't believe that, you are saying His dying was not enough for you. But there is no greater sacrifice than for the perfect Son of God to give up His life as a ransom for you, for all of us. Talk about amazing grace!

Expectations

On a personal note, what are my expectations of marriage? Why in the world would I even think about doing that again after two failed marriages and subsequent pain-filled divorces? I truly enjoyed being married. I loved having my spouse come home for dinner, talk about our days, and then holding his hand when I fell asleep. I loved having someone who I couldn't wait to share good news with or have someone to comfort me when I was sad. I enjoyed cooking dinner for my family and keeping up the house (most of the time). I loved our annual Christmas shopping excursions and finding the perfect gift for him. But to get a true picture of marriage, I have to also remember the things that drove me crazy such as the walking on eggshells so I wouldn't upset him, or the back-ache from the stress of not knowing what kind of mood he'd be in. That wasn't necessarily his fault, and one major lesson I have learned is to not let other people's mood affect me to that extent.

One of our DivorceCare[2] facilitators talked about learning from the way we chose to respond in our marriages. Wow, that is deep, and when I think back he is so right. If I had responded differently in many situations, my marriage might still be in tact. I have a tendency to close up when I've been hurt. What if instead when my feelings were hurt by my spouse, I had gone to him and calmly told him he had hurt my feelings and why. What would have happened if instead of him feeling he always took a back seat and not telling me how he felt, if he would have told me? I could have worked on ways to truly show my respect for him. What if I would have more effectively communicated I desired to spend time with him and asked him to have a date night with me once a week or so? So, I can learn from this. Now I need to choose to respond more honestly with my children and friends.

Another freeing thought I learned from the DivorceCare[2] class is that divorce is an occurrence in my life, but it does not have to define me! It is a sin and we need to repent, and even learn from it. But we can lay it at the feet of Christ and He forgives us and throws it into the deepest sea never to be remembered by Him again. Then each day we can remember the verse in Romans 8:1, "*There is no condemnation for those in Christ*!" Amen! Quite possibly, God will use you and this painful event in your life to help others through theirs. No one can minister to a divorced woman better than another divorced woman.

Lord, I stand amazed at You! Help me remember You are always with me, to be totally content in my singleness and to remember each day Your love and sacrifice for me and truly know You are more than enough for me.

Thursday, October 19, 2006

Last night I continued to read *Pursuing Your Life Dream* by Eastman Curtis. He talked about the importance of remaining faithful in the little things and about David and how he was called by God. David then went back to attending the sheep, as that was his job. This really hit me because I am excited about this book and all that God may do with it, and I can see great things happening through my "spiritual eyes." Sometimes it is hard to continue to live my "normal" life – go to work, clean the house, go to the grocery. This was the perfect reminder for me. Not that I would have ever stopped doing those things, as I've always been responsible and maybe even anal, but I needed to remember to be faithful and to do them and everything I do (even the mundane) as if doing them to the Lord. God may be testing me to see how faithful I am in the little things in life before He allows me to experience grander things. Oh how I pray to be faithful in all I do. Mr. Curtis said God is looking for faithful men and women.[41]

October 26, 2006

In this week's DivorceCare class workbook[42], I was led to a very comforting verse in Isaiah. Isaiah 54:5 says, *"For your Maker is your husband – the Lord almighty is His name – the Holy One of Israel is your Redeemer."* Wow! I love this. I can say, "I have the most amazing husband in the world! In fact, He created the world." You can say this too! I can't help but think of the references throughout the Bible of Christ as the Bridegroom. I usually think of the church as a whole as

His bride, but how personally comforting to know He also means I am his bride!

This got me to thinking about the roles a husband usually plays in our lives and how they compare with Christ's promises to us. First, the husband is a **protector**, as we ladies like to feel secure. Isaiah 41:13 says, "*For I am the Lord your God, who takes hold of your right hand and says to you, Do not fear; I will help you.*" A husband is also usually the main breadwinner or **provider** so we can clothe and feed our families, and in Matthew 6 it talks about God as our provider specifically meeting these very needs. We also want our husband to **love us** like no other and to be forever **committed** to us. In Psalm 52:5b it says, "*I will trust in God's unfailing love for ever and ever.*" His love is the perfect love, without fear, and lasts for eternity! Praise Him!

We also desire **companionship** with our husband; we long to spend time talking with him, getting to know him and doing fun things and laugh together. God has this covered, too. He is always with us. We can't see him with our physical eyes (but some day we will) and sometimes when we need someone "with skin on" we need only look for someone He has sent into our life. This can be another woman friend to shop with (men don't seem to enjoy this anyway). But if you'll seek Him, you'll undoubtedly feel His presence in your heart. You can talk to Him all throughout the day and He listens (and He isn't just listening during the commercials at half-time). He delights in giving you peace and joy in your heart. But as in a successful marriage, this relationship requires two-way dialogue, work and commitment. He will always be there for you, but He wants to hear from you every day, not just when things are bad. He wants you to appreciate all He has done for you and to see him in unexpected places and circumstances. He wants you to desire to spend time with Him.

My quiet time really began when my husband left. Before that, I was in church, leading a middle school small group, attending Bible study and I prayed a lot. I had a relationship with Christ, but at bedtime when I was alone after Brady left, I decided this would be my quiet time, and it has been a blessing! I look forward to it each day. It has been incredible how many times I read a passage from scripture and the very next day hear someone talking about it on the radio, in church, or recognize it in a song. I smile whenever this happens, as I think it is a message from God letting me know I am exactly where He wants me at that moment in time. How amazing the God of creation would even bother with just little ole me, but He does, because He delights in His children.

Completion

If you are single again and contemplating re-marriage, I would urge you to think about what it is you're truly seeking. Are you lonely? Are you looking for someone to take away the pain you feel? Are you seeking someone to give you the unconditional love you missed in childhood? Are you looking for another person to make you complete? It is important to realize another person will not complete you, especially if they, too, are incomplete. [42]

For a marriage to be successful, it requires two **complete** individuals. This doesn't mean each is perfect. Instead it means they both continue to work on themselves, making themselves the best people they can be, who God designed them to be. They are healthy and can stand on their own.

Often times, we think we need to look for the right person, but instead it is imperative we focus on *becoming* the right person. Statistics show that if we aren't content being single, we probably won't be content when married.

If you are feeling incomplete, find out what you are missing. Are you feeling unloved, not cherished, unattractive, unprotected? Pray about this, and our God in Heaven will comfort you and guide you. I want you to know to the depths of your soul that God loves you so much, you are beautiful in His sight and you are precious to Him. Only He can complete you.

Also, I would encourage you to stop looking for Mr. Right, and to focus on the possibility that God could want you all to himself right now, just as my friend told me. Maybe He isn't ready to share you with a guy right now. When we have a boyfriend, we tend to spend just about all of our extra time with him and God gets the leftovers. Maybe He has a lesson for you, such as patience, contentment or complete reliance on Him. Maybe He wants you to discover who He created you to be, and to tell you of the special plan He has for your life, a plan no one else can accomplish.

Sometimes I find myself daydreaming about "Mr. Right" saying I'm beautiful or stunning. I think most women desire to feel this way. We are bombarded with beautiful women on television or in the movies, and we can often believe we fall short. It is amazing to know when God looks at us, He says, "beautiful" because He looks at our hearts. When we are in His word and giving ourselves to Him with the desire to truly do His will in our lives, we are beautiful. We are reflecting Him and that can't stay inside, it shines through us and touches others. In Psalms 27:4 it says, "*One thing I ask from the LORD, this only do I seek: that I may dwell in the house of the LORD all the days of my life, to gaze on the beauty of the LORD and to seek Him in his temple."*

Lord, my prayer continues to be that I will exude You in all I do and all I am. My heart is overflowing with awe and gratitude for all You are and all You continue to do in my life. I am blessed immensely and I praise You for all You have done and for all You will do through me.

Learning from Teaching

One of the advantages of teaching Sunday school, besides the obvious of getting to know some fun young people, is I am also learning as I prepare the lessons. This week we talked about Noah. Most of us know that story, but I had forgotten about the words "*Noah walked with God*" in Genesis 6:9. I love that. It made me ask myself, "Am I doing that? What does that even look like?" I think it means each day we just simply talk to Him throughout the day; when we notice a beautiful sunrise, we thank Him for creating that, or when we make it safely to our destination, we thank Him for that. Or when we see someone hurting, we comfort and pray for them.

In the story of Noah, because he was a righteous man (not perfect, but he walked with God), he and his family were spared from the destruction of the earth and all that was in it. God was going to send a flood to wipe out the evil that had permeated it. So God gave him specific instructions (which had to sound ludicrous) to build an ark so they'd be safe from the rain He was going to send on the earth for 40 days. Can you imagine Noah's neighbors remarks? "Hey, Noah, what in the world are you building? Oh, God told you he is going to send rain, right? What is rain anyway? I don't think our neighborhood association allows that big monstrosity being built in your yard. What an eye-sore." Can you image what Mrs. Noah had to be hearing from her women-friends when they got together at Bunco? And what about his sons, Shem, Ham and Japheth? They probably were ridiculed by their peers. I wonder if they supported Noah from the beginning of the construction? I have to believe they backed him up since he was walking with God, that they probably saw evidence of God's goodness in their everyday lives.

The lesson here for me is **even when something seems impossible or too big for me, if it is from God, He'll be faithful to see the task through**. This is exactly what I needed to hear. I believe with all my heart this book is from God, but I have really been questioning myself. Is it really from Him or is it just something I want to do? If I am truly walking with God, He'll give me all the instructions, just like He gave the *exact* dimensions and material information to Noah. He'll guide me and will open the proper doors and will shine His favor on me in His time.

November 19, 2006

Today at church, one of the coolest things happened to me. I went in to the fellowship hall, as I do every Sunday between services, to help with the middle school/high school students until time for their Sunday school class to start. Barb and Stan, two friends and leaders of my small group, had a gift for me. They said God is going to use me, and they wanted to thank me for helping them and their friend who was going through a divorce. They had emailed Chris Tomlin's manager about how they wanted to do something nice for me, and that I was a huge fan. They asked for a life-size cutout of him (how funny is that!). The manager informed them he didn't have any of those, but would send an autographed photograph instead. Today, they gave me the framed autographed photo. Having an autographed photo complete with my name on it was amazing, but the thought that went behind this just blew me away. What incredible friends God has given me!

December 1, 2006

On my way to work this morning, the sky was amazing. It was filled with dark snow storm clouds moving briskly across the sky, but at one point I could see a sunny spot on top. It made me think about my life the last couple of years. The pain and uncertainly of my divorce covered my "sky" with dark storm clouds, but though I could not see it yet, God was already shining his love and light on me. Now it has totally broken through and fills my heart. I want The Son to shine through me to others weathering the pain and seemingly hopelessness of divorce.

Lord, You know my heart and its desire, as I believe You put it there. Help me to truly be a light, a glimmer of hope to hurting people. Please guide me each day in action and with the words I speak.

Today, one of my bosses told me about the possibility of hiring a property manager to help me. Wow! Just yesterday I was thinking that if I have success with this book, I may need to travel some to promote it. I may only be able to work part-time on some days, and may need to find someone who can run the office of a commercial real estate office in my absence.

Lord, this makes me both excited and nervous. I love my job and I can't imagine not being here full-time, but I know I need to hold on loosely and listen for Your guidance. When it comes to finances, this is the hardest area of faith for me because I'm not sure where the line between being responsible and a good steward and faith is. Lord, help me to be a better steward now and to work extremely hard on getting debt paid off. Help me to be so in tune with You on this scary issue, knowing Your plan will be best for me and that You will continue to provide for me.

December 4, 2006

Tonight at the DivorceCare class, I was reminded my *purpose* is not marriage. The professionals on the DVD explained marriage can be a wonderful blessing and important **part** of our life, but our purpose is about so much more.[43] God has a purpose for each of us. Also, after some reflection, I think I've figured out that my desire to be married is out of the desire to be loved by the perfect love. But what I need to remember is that I already am! No matter who my spouse may be some day (if that is God's plan), he won't love me as God does. And I won't be able to love him as completely as God can. It's not that he or I wouldn't desire to do that, but we aren't God, so we just aren't capable of His perfect love.

Lord, help me to consider my singleness as a gift, one that allows me to focus more on Your plans than if I were married. Please allow me to be content and to grow into the woman You created me to be, finding my purpose in Your plan. I stand amazed that You would be interested in bothering with me. But I know I am one of Your precious children and You have only good things in store for me. Praise You. Amen.

December 25, 2006 1:48 am

It's Christmas morning, and I'm about to get a few hours of sleep but wanted to write a couple of thoughts from today.

First, from the lesson I taught in Sunday school class yesterday: It talked about Joseph's plans to wed Mary and how those plans, even though good, were interrupted. I learned as I make plans, I need to be sure to watch for what God is doing in my midst, and be ready for an interruption.

The second brought tears to my eyes in church today, as our minister asked us what we wanted more than anything. He suggested peace (which I already have), joy (I already have that too) but then he suggested love – the love that will not leave you or trade you in on a newer model. This touched my heart and brought tears to my eyes. I know I am loved by God and I am truly thankful for that, but there is still that desire in my heart to have someone special love me and cherish me and long to be with me. And what I've discovered is I don't have to feel bad about having that desire in my heart, because I think God Himself put it there. I wonder if Jesus experienced this feeling when He was on earth or was He so close to our Heavenly Father that He truly met all His desires? Because He knew the perfect love of God, maybe that was all He needed and desired.

Lord, thank You it is not wrong to long for someone. I remember the promise that if I will delight in You, You will give me the desires of my heart. Maybe You're working out all the details even as I write this.

Lord, I am excited, but somewhat nervous about the New Year. I'm excited because You have promised me an abundant life, but nervous because the book project is way bigger than me, but that is how I'll know it is truly from You. In fact, I'm reading and studying "The

Prayer of Jabez"[44] *and it encourages us to do something so big that without God in it, it will fail. Happy Birthday, Lord. Thank you for humbling yourself to come to us and to live amongst us and experience what we feel. I offer You myself and am humbled to think You would even consider me worthy of Your love, concern and provision. Lord, I want You to truly be the love of my life.*

I once told my husband I had a fear of abandonment. After being left by two husbands, I guess I don't need to fear that anymore. Now I just hate it. After all, I believe fear comes from not knowing about something and being scared of it. Unfortunately, I know all too well the feelings that go along with being left. I think this is why the words "I will never leave you nor forsake you" spoken by God has had such a huge impact on me. Knowing the God who created everything has promised to stay with me no matter what, is one of the most comforting thoughts I can have. And He has been with me through it all. Christ knows the feeling of being abandoned, too, all too well.

XIII

God Gave Me A Song

December 30, 2006

On about December 22, I picked up my *Prayer of Jabez* [56] book that my good friend, Lenisa, had given me for my birthday about eight years ago. I'd looked through it before but it really spoke to me this time. In fact this will be my prayer for 2007: that God will enlarge my territory. As I write this, I can't help but wonder if God "blessed" me with a song yesterday as I was working at my desk. One minute I was paying invoices, and the next minute I was humming and singing to myself words of praise. Before I knew it, I'd typed them up and even sang it into my own voicemail box so I wouldn't forget how it went. (Thankfully, no one was in the office, because I'm not sure how I would have explained it!) Hello, where did this come from? Is this what songwriters refer to when they say "God gave them a song?"

During this holiday season, I've been thinking about the New Year, and wondering what it will hold for me. I am both excited and scared. I wonder who I'll meet and what I'll get to do. Will I write the book? Will it be good? Will it get published? Will it be helpful to someone? Additionally, will I get to speak? What will the girls be doing this time next year?

Sunday, January 7, 2007

It has been a while since I've journaled, and there are several thoughts in my head that I need to write down.

1. I'm reading a book entitled *The Journey of Desire* [45] by John Eldredge, and I'm learning to think more about Heaven and what it will really be like so I can get excited about it. I mean, I've gotten more excited about my new car and Kitchen-aid mixer than I do about Heaven. I'm realizing that maybe what I do in this life matters a little less – who cares if I make a fool of myself if I believe I'm stepping out in faith?
2. I think God gave me a song called "I Stand Amazed," but I'm not sure what to do with it.

So Lord, I'm asking for your guidance. Your word says, "I do not have because I do not ask." So Lord, I am pleading for Your guidance and wisdom. Help me to not run ahead or lag behind You – but to be in Your timing. Lord, again if a song comes from this, it will be so obviously from You, as I'm no songwriter . . . I can't even READ music!

Tonight at small group, we looked at John 15, "The vine and the branches" and I had a thought. In verse 2 it says,

"*He cuts off every branch in me that bares no fruit.*" I can't help but think of my ex-husband. Did God literally cut him out of my life because he was cutting off some of my fruit-bearing potential? I love this whole illustration and reminder that I need to stay attached to The Life Source to bear fruit, and the Holy Spirit is like the rain and sun that helps sustain me in this production. God is the gardener, pruning so more fruit can come forth, and even though some of those cuts may be painful, they are always for our own good. Just as a gardener has an ultimate purpose for his vineyard and the fruit it produces, God has an ultimate purpose for each of "his branches."

Lord, I want nothing more than to know and live in Your perfect plan You have predestined for me. If that plan includes a book and/or song and/or speaking, so be it, but I pray for Your blessing and for Your hand of power and courage to be upon me and for protection from temptation and evil.

After attending all thirteen classes of the DivorceCare[2] program, I felt led to become a facilitator. So after several training classes, my first time co-facilitating with this ministry is tomorrow night. I'm nervous.

Help me to say what You want me to say, to know when to listen, and to comfort where needed. I pray especially for my new friend, Karen, and all those who will attend the class tomorrow night. Give them courage to come and find healing in You.

January 9, 2007 – notes from conversation with my phone counselor, Debbie

- Have a dating advisory committee in mind for when I start dating
- Schedule time for writing

- OK to chill out some
- Be sure to have some fun
- Suggested I start a journal to chronicle at least one thing a day that is evidence of God. She said in pretty much all her notes from our conversations, I've had a story about something being from God.
- She said dating is the hardest thing she has ever done.
- She is glad I am not defining myself as single by doing only single things, but instead am involved with the youth and going out with married couples, too.
- She said I've done an amazing job healing . . . that I've worked hard.

Saturday, January 13, 2007

Tonight I went to the Winter Jam Concert with some friends. Steven Curtis Chapman and Jeremy Camp were especially great! Jeremy Camp said when he was writing songs, his prayer was God would give him something to touch the peoples' hearts. Then he realized instead, he was to touch God's heart and He would do the rest. (So as I type this today, I just heard his new song and the lyrics say, *"Lord we just want to touch your heart."* [43]) Wow.

God, I want that. I want to touch Your heart with my life. Please guide me. How do I know if this song is from You? Is it because I can't get it out of my head? Does that mean it is from You? Why am I so nervous? Tonight I was really touched by the lyrics, "I will walk by faith," [48] from one of Jeremy Camp's songs. *Lord, is my faith lacking? I don't want it to – I just don't know how to tell what is from You and what are my desires. Please help me to know and to act upon it. I don't want to have any regrets, so why am I afraid? Who cares if people think I'm crazy – You will always love me. You want me to dream big because You are a big God and nothing is impossible for You!*

Lord God, I ask for a clear sign from You that I am to record the song. I love you and long to serve You and bring joy to Your heart.

Sunday, January 14, 2007

Today's sermon was entitled, "Come Follow Me" and my minister Rick explained how Jesus called his disciples to come "now." They left their boats and even left their father, Zebedee, in the boat to follow Christ. He explained the "now" reveals our faith and trust and our priorities. Wow! I could not get the song, and what to do with it, off my mind!

Lord, is this Your answer? Do You want me to act on it now?

Rick went on to explain when we follow Jesus, we need to be OK with leaving security. I can't help but think of eventually working part-time at my current job (which I love) to promote my book. This sounds so outrageous, but if this is what God has destined for me, then OK. But I am nervous just thinking about the possibility. (Secretly I'm excited too.)

Then Rick explained how when we are obedient to Christ, He rewards us big time! Just like when the fishermen's nets broke and the boat began to sink because of the large number of fish after Peter obeyed and put the nets back out into the waters at Jesus' request. Rick also said we will have big adventure when we follow Christ, now. Yes, I'm ready!

Monday, January 15, 2007

This morning I emailed PJ, our Music Minister, about recording the song at church. He responded kindly he'd be happy to help me, and he'd even be willing to put music to it. I was nervous in emailing him and explained that I know it sounds ridiculous that God would give **me** a song. I even asked him to not tell anyone so I wouldn't look foolish to too many people. His response was so encouraging. He said it is never foolish to follow where we think God is leading, and that it is also scary. Now we are just working on scheduling a time to record it.

Lord, please bless these efforts. Please make my voice pure and beautiful, and calm my nerves. Help me remember the words came from my heart and I long for them to exalt, honor and please You, just as Jeremy Camp told us at the Winter Jam concert.

Today, my sister-in-law, Donna, called and told me the kindest thing. She said if she could be like anybody in the world, she'd want to be like me! She said when she is around me, she feels like she can do anything! This is probably the nicest compliment I've ever received. Then, she said, "I love you" at the end of our phone conversation. Wow! Lord, thank You. Hopefully I am imitating You and that is whom she longs to be like. Help me in all I say and do. What a blessing! (And I love her, too.)

January 26, 2007

Today's thought is about beauty – I hope we get more beautiful as we age because we have spent more time with God. He is molding us into His image, and we can't help but have this inner transformation shape our appearance. After all, I've heard it said that beauty is the very essence of God. I love that!

January 27, 2007

Today I recorded my song! Note the date – **it is exactly two years after my husband left me, and I recorded a song!** I just recorded an acapella version in an office at church, not in a fancy studio, but I stepped out in faith and did it.

I arrived at church around noon and went into the office set up for me. I was so thankful I was allowed to do this in private. After taking a couple of deep breaths, and saying a prayer, I recorded it. It was not perfect, but I was pleased with it after only one take (for a non-professional).

I walked out into the front office area to say "hi" to one of my best friends, LuAnn, who is the church secretary. That is when the date hit me like a ton of bricks. Two years ago to the day, I had come to church and stood in the very same place. All of a sudden the memories came rushing back of a broken, hurting woman looking for comfort, looking for answers, looking for hope. Tears came to my eyes (and to hers) but unlike last time, these were tears of joy, tears of thankfulness that God had been with me every step of the way and had not only healed my broken heart, but He gave me a new **song to sing**!

Lord, your healing power is truly amazing! Thank You so much for being right with me through all the pain, tears, shame, questioning myself and heartache. I know You did not enjoy me being in that desperate state. I believe as I grieved, You grieved. You are that personal. However, I think You just kept thinking, "You hold on, my dear child, for I still have a plan for your life and you just need to persevere through this and when you have healed, I will reveal an abundant life that you can't even begin to imagine."

I couldn't help but remember the spring break mission trip in April of 2005 when I was at a crossroads not knowing where my life would go, feeling it was in my husband's hands and control, when our Youth Minister said to me, "No matter what happens, God is still in control and you will have a *song to sing*." He was right and I'm anxious to see what God will do with it. The lyrics are as follows:

I stand amazed, at your presence, Lord. I stand amazed, at your love.
I stand amazed, at your awesomeness. I stand amazed at who you are.

Chorus: *You are the Lord of lord, and King of kings,*
Yet somehow the son of man.
You are the Savior of the world, I know,
Yet you guide my every plan.

I stand amazed, at your peace, O Lord. I stand amazed at your grace.
I stand amazed at your healing power, and I long to seek your face.
I stand amazed at your purpose, Lord, that You came as a humble babe
I stand amazed when I think about the cross and the ultimate price You paid.

I don't yet know what God's intention for this song is. Maybe He has grand plans for it, but maybe He just gave it to me so I can sing it to Him each night as I stand in my kitchen before going to bed. I guess time will tell. (Note: A link to the song is available at Annette8788.wordpress.com.)

Wednesday, January 31, 2007

Lord, I just want to do Your will but I am so inept and don't want to mess up or disappoint You. So I pray my obedience brings delight to Your heart, but even more so my faith in You and Your awesome power to do the impossible brings You joy in me. I want to become beautiful from the inside out. I want to exude You in all I do. I want You, God, to be the love of my life. Please help me where I am weak.

February 3, 2007

I'm reading a great book entitled, *Captivating* [46] by Stasi & John Eldredge, and I suggest every woman read it. Apparently God finds me captivating! And, I believe if God has given me a song, He wants it sung, so He'll guide me in getting it to the artist of His choosing in His timing. (What if it is me after all?)

February 5, 2007

This week's theme for me has been stepping out in faith, being vulnerable as that is how God made me – to not be afraid of being who I am and if I am rejected (again) I'll still be OK. Oh, it will hurt, but I need to remember I do not get my sense of worth from other people's perceptions or opinion of me. Instead I must have the confidence in knowing God does not reject me at all and as His child, He delights in me.

Today I put in a Mark Schultz CD. The first song I listened to is called "You Are A Child Of Mine." [47] It is a beautiful song and I've heard it numerous times before, but tonight is the first time I'd ever picked up on the following lyrics: "*So I listen as You tell me who I am and* ***who it is I'm gonna be****. And I hang on every word knowing I have heard that I am loved and I am free.*" I love this!

Lord, am I going to be a songwriter, recording artist, speaker and author bringing Your hope to some of those hurting? What a daunting task but one that only You could guide me to and through. I am speechless thinking about this. I don't deserve this sort of favor at all. But Lord, I only want to do Your will, so please guide me each day. I don't want to be foolish and take things into my own hands. I need You daily, Lord, so speak to me. Help my hearts desires become only what Your heart's desire is for me. Thank you that I am a child of the most high King!

Sunday, February 25, 2007

Rick's sermon today was on John 9:1–12, Jesus healing the blind man. Here are some notes that especially spoke to me:

- The Lord gives us joy when we are obedient
- **Obedience delayed is disobedience**
- God's power is displayed in our weakness
- I need to rely on God's grace versus my ability
- Faith requires us to be obedient
- The power of God is discovered through obedience
- - Jesus said, "Those who obey my commands love me and my love remains in them".

Jesus said, "Those who obey my commands love me and my love remains in them".

- Standing for truth requires boldness. Almost immediately after the blind man was healed, he was questioned about Jesus. I love how he answered, "This I know, I was blind, but now I see." I could use that same idea – I was broken but now am healed.
- He then worshipped Jesus.
- Jesus heard the man had been thrown out so He went to him. How like Jesus to show such compassion. He really does meet us where we are.

Monday, March 5, 2007

Tuesday, February 27, through Sunday, March 4, I was in Orlando, Florida visiting Nickie, who has been there attending the Disney College Program since mid-January. It was a great trip! I stayed with Whitney and her family, and enjoyed them so much. I have to admit, though, I had some mixed emotions during my visit. I cried when I saw "my little girl" all by herself waiting for me at the baggage-claim area. She looked so grown up – like a young woman. I have missed her so much.

I laughed until I cried on numerous occasions with Nickie and her friends as we spent time at The Magic Kingdom.

I felt a little lonely on a couple of occasions wishing I had a husband to love me and hold my hand, (especially watching the families at Blizzard Beach). Seeing Whitney's relationship with her husband and how he interacted with her and the children made me long for that.

At church on Sunday, I was sad thinking how I'd be leaving Nickie in a couple of hours, but I was also so thankful for all God has done for me that I cried . . . again. The sermon was on thankfulness and praying with thanksgiving. It was wonderful.

Tuesday March 6, 2007

Today I spoke with my phone counselor, Debbie. She told me the first time she talked to me was two years ago on March 7, 2005. She said I have come a long way! Thank You, Lord!

I told her about the song I recorded and she loved it. Especially that I recorded it on the two-year anniversary of Brady leaving. She loved the fact I was obedient to what I believed God wanted me to do.

She then said something I can't get out of my mind. She said, "Ask Him for more songs." Wow! I'd never thought of that, but I love the idea! After all, He is truly the great composer, the creator of music itself. To think God would even bother with me is mind-boggling and humbling, but so amazing and exciting! God, my life is in Your hands.

We talked about my emotions while I was in Florida, and she said it is normal and is part of the grieving, especially while staying with Whitney and longing for such a partnership. She called Whitney a "divinely-appointed friend" and she prayed for more of those for me!

Debbie told me about the coolest vision she has regarding a mate. She envisions herself in one of God's hands and a mate in the other hand, and when God brings

His hands together, He would bring them together. I love that! She explained there is a difference between a date and a mate.

We talked about the fact that I am complete as a single woman, but in Florida it still hurt some wanting a mate. She said I have a talent for writing, too; I paint a picture with my words. Cool!

Thursday, March 8, 2007

Today on the way to work, I listened to Bob Russell preach via the radio. He touched on several things I'd heard or read within just the last two days.

1. "The sheep know the sound of the Shepherd's voice." Oh how I long for this.
2. "The devil is like a roaring lion wanting to devour." Rick preached on this just last night.
3. "Wives submit to your husbands." We talked about submission during The Truth Project on Tuesday night, and when we do that, we are honoring the Bridegroom of the Church.

Lord, what does it mean when I get so many messages like this? Is that your kind voice letting me know I am where I am supposed to be?

Please guide me today and each day to work for You and work toward becoming the woman You want me to be – the woman You created me to be.

Lord, tonight I realized the most important thing I am called to do is to be a witness for You – there are more important things than me being satisfied and happy while on earth. I know You want me to be full of joy and blessed because You are my loving Father, and just as

I want that for my children, You want that for me, too. But I think if I am in Your will each day, then joy from You will be in me naturally. Please guide me each day in Your perfect plan. I don't doubt You, but I do doubt myself at times.

Sunday, April 1, 2007

Today is my 42nd birthday! My Sunday school class gave me a card that touched my heart. One of the students wrote I make coming to church fun, and one said it is obvious I am living my life for God's glory and that I've had an influence on his life.

Lord, I feel so blessed to know these students. You know my desire is to live my life to glorify You. Help me to realize what a gift it is to teach these young hearts.

Tuesday, April 10, 2007

Since the guys I work with are on vacation this week, I brought some CD's to listen to as 9 hours of silence would drive me crazy. What a blessing it has been. Today I listened to Hillsong's United CD[51] and here are a couple of thoughts I love.

1. One of the youth leaders at Hillsong's church in Sydney Australia said, "Jesus said He was leaving but He would leave the Holy Spirit with us and *we'll do greater works than He did through His power*." Wow!
2. One of the guys in the band said, "There will be a new song as long as people are being saved. The new songs will stop when it becomes about the new songs."

3. Another person talked about "listening to God's voice." This seems to be a reoccurring theme for me this week. Last night, one of the facilitators at the Divorce Recovery Class talked about this. He said God doesn't usually tell us where to go like we want to hear, but instead He tells us to come to Him, rest, listen and have faith that He'll lead us. The facilitator said, "God always wants to speak to us."

Oh Lord, how I want to truly listen. Help me to hear You when You speak to me. Help that to be my passion, to truly listen for You and not wonder about what You'll do with the song You gave me, but instead rest in Your arms knowing that I've put it at Your feet to use as You wish, to bring You glory, to touch Your heart. I believe I was obedient to Your leading so help me to rest in that.

This morning I heard Kyle Idleman preaching on the radio on Acts. He talked about "the Spirit's leading" and how it is too mysterious to break down into a 30-minute message, but it is powerful and we'll know His leading. He talked about how Phillip (I think) was led to the Ethiopian Eunuch and how he listened to the man instead of preaching at him. He called this meeting a "divine-appointment." Kyle talked about being obedient to God's leading. He also explained that usually God leads us out of our comfort zone.

On this topic of "leading," I've been feeling I am supposed to take the Divorce Recovery program I attended last year and help facilitate now at SECC, to my home church. I met with one of my ministers about this and found out the coolest thing. He told me another lady in our congregation (whom I had not met) just came to him *this week* with the same idea! Coincidence? I don't think so. I think this was God's design and maybe I really did listen to His leading!

So Yvonne and I met, and I felt like I'd known her for years. A class is in the works. (Note: Yvonne has become one of my dearest friends.)

July 2007

I haven't journaled for a couple of months because my family has been dealing with a tragedy. My first husband (the father of my children) died unexpectedly in April, so obviously this has been a difficult time. Watching my daughters grieve has been so hard, because I can't do a thing to fix it and make it better, which is part of what a mom is supposed to do, or so we think. So on top of the other losses they have experienced, they have another one to deal with at their young ages. I hate it. If I could do something to take their pain away, I would do it in a heartbeat!

Lord, please comfort them, his parents, siblings and other friends and family members.

August 2007

This week, our DivorceCare[2] Recovery class started at my home church, and it went great. There are no "sign-ups" so we didn't know if anyone would show up, but they did! We have about 10 attending, which is really the perfect number of people for us. We have a male facilitator helping, too, which is so important since almost half of our class is men. After watching a DVD, everyone shared their stories. Oh, there is so much pain and hurt in here, but I guess that means there is a lot of great work for God to do.

XIV

A Dream Comes True

Tuesday, August 28, 2007

Today I told my phone counselor about all the good things going on in my life. I have this excitement and joy in my heart for which I am so thankful. I told her I feel my life is so fulfilling that I don't need to date. I am content but do have moments when I long for a mate. I know my life is in God's hands so, like Tony Evans said in the Divorce Care video, "Seek the Lord, and He'll find your mate." [48] I love that!

I also told her about one of my dreams coming true. Let me explain. The head of a missionary organization in Poland came to the States for a missionary presentation and reception. Maui came to our office on Friday to meet with Stan (one of my bosses, who is also the President of this organization state-side). They discussed several issues and then met with me to go over the financial reports, since I volunteer by taking care of their accounting here. Before we began, he asked me to be on the Board of Directors (and said there was only one correct answer, "yes"). What an honor!

Then, he shocked me by asking me to **speak at the woman's conference** in Poland next year! Hello! This is one of my dreams! And I get to go to another country! How incredible is that? But here is the coolest part, the part where God, the all-powerful Creator is so personal. The reason this all came about is because Stan had sent Maui a copy of the "God Is In Control" talk I gave to the middle school/high school girls in February 2006 – the talk that Trina read to Angie in March of that same year – and Maui read it and asked me to speak! He said I have a powerful testimony, and I really believe I do. Thank You, Lord!

God, I am humbled at how very personal You are. I am like a vaporette in comparison to Your creation, yet You see me, You know me, You love me and You have a plan You created just for me!

My phone counselor, Debbie, reminded me today it is important to totally **surrender** and ask God what He wants me to do; not just pray for my desires. She told me to put those aside and listen for His voice, to seek His plan.

So Lord, I do that now. You know the dreams and desires in my heart, and I know if they are from You, that You will bring them to fruition in your perfect timing.

My First Experience with Dating

In November, almost three years since my husband left, I felt I was ready to start dating. So, over the period of a couple of months, I went on several dates with a really nice guy I met in a class at church. I was really enjoying the conversation and company, and I believed he was too. Then, suddenly, nothing. He did not call or email. It was as if he fell off the face of the earth. After a month of nothing, I sent him a short email just to be sure he hadn't died, disguised as a "Happy Birthday" message. He responded, thanking me for remembering his birthday and said he was busy with life, and he'd met someone over the Christmas holidays. Ouch! But here is an idea: be a man and just tell me instead of not communicating like a coward! That is what happens in the dating world. That is why I probably am not quite ready for it, because it felt like another personal rejection – like I had been dumped again. Maybe I'm not as recovered as I thought I was.

And, once again, it hurt. I began to wonder all over again, what is wrong with me? Why am I not enough for a guy? Why is it so easy for them to walk away from me? Do they ever miss me? (And I'll admit that I wondered why, for once, I can't be the dumper? I digress.) I realized I just wanted to be loved, and I really liked the idea of having someone think I was special. This guy was so complimentary, and since encouraging words is my love language, he was really meeting my needs by building up my self-esteem . . . well, while he was speaking to me, anyway.

I needed to remind myself that having a boyfriend (or husband) does not make me complete. I am complete just as I am. It is not wrong to have this desire for companionship, as I believe God made us that way. But I need to be content with myself knowing if God's plan for me includes a mate (or even just a date), He will bring that about in His time. I often get frustrated with myself because I know all of this stuff in my head, but wonder why I can't truly get it into my heart.

I have no regrets about this failed dating situation, as it has been a learning experience for me. First off, I have learned I need to research dating and how to do it. You see, I didn't date much at all when I was younger; I just married the guys. I am technically a decade or so behind. But the most important thing I learned is I need to look inside of myself and see what sort of guys I attract and why. I need to continue to work on myself, making myself the best person I can be. That will attract healthy men. Of course, I also know God may call me to be single for the rest of my life. If that is His plan for me, I know it is for the best. Now my prayer is if that is truly His will, I'll truly be able to look at my singleness as a gift and a blessing and be not just content, but thrive in it. Again, I often have to remind my heart of this.

April 2008

After months of meetings and preparing with five other ladies (who are wonderful) and writing and practicing two talks, it was time to go to Zakosciele, Poland to assist the Polish team with their annual women's conference. What an honor. I am so humbled to be part of this. Each of us presented two different sessions at both three-day conferences. I met so many amazing ladies and learned that even though we live in different countries and speak different languages, we have the same concerns and desires. I got to meet with several adorable ladies one-on-one who shared their heart-breaking stories of rejection and divorce. I was able to pray with them and hopefully encourage them about God's healing power and love.

My understanding is that in their culture, people just don't open up and share the personal stuff of their lives, so that seems to be the attraction with having us American women come to the conference. Even though most need a translator, it is refreshing for them to hear us share our stories and give them hope. At least that is our goal.

April 2009

I went to my second women's conference in Poland earlier this month, and one of my talks was about forgiveness. It is an important topic, so I've included part of my presentation:

Reflecting God through Forgiveness

I am truly honored to be here in Poland with you all, and when I heard what the theme of this conference is, I was so thankful because I knew I would get the opportunity to tell you about a gift God gave me . . . you could call it an early Christmas present. Let me give you a brief explanation of my past and then I'll "unwrap" the gift for you. (I went on to explain how my husband left, etc.)

So a few months later he filed for divorce and I cried and questioned and grieved. I remember just barely having the energy to go to work and when I got home, I'd throw myself across the bed and cry my eyes out. I remember telling God, "I can't even pray right now . . . I haven't the words to say or the energy to say them." But I believe that God knew what I wanted to pray. In Psalm 139 verse 2, it says, "*You know when I sit down and when I stand up. You know my thoughts even when I am far away.*" I love Psalm 139! It is one of my favorite passages and I read it over and over again during this time because I needed God's truth to over-ride the negative messages I was telling myself. My favorite part is verses 17 & 18. "*How precious are your thoughts about me, O God. I can't even count them; they outnumber the grains of sand! . .*" Just think about that. God thinks about you more times than there are grains of sand on the beaches! Amazing!

So after working really hard on healing for about two years, attending a Divorce Recovery workshop, going to counseling, and spending time with God and in His word almost every night before I went to sleep, I eventually knew I had to forgive my ex-husband. I knew it was what God wanted me to do and I wanted to be like Christ.

See, Christ forgave in the midst of the most horrific of circumstances. He had been beaten beyond recognition with whips that actually had pieces of bone and hooks on them that would tear the flesh on his back. A crown of thorns had mockingly been smashed into his forehead piercing his skin causing blood to trickle down His face. He had been spit upon, was striped, and nails were driven through his hands and feet into a rugged wooden cross. I can't even image such physical pain, and yet before he died, He said the most unbelievable words . . . "*Father forgive them, they know not what they are doing,*" according to Luke 23:34. Wow, that is amazing! If Christ can forgive among the most unbearable pain and circumstances, then certainly I could forgive too.

Now let me say here that **forgiveness is NOT saying that what someone did to us was OK.** No. It is always wrong when a person abuses another. It was wrong for my husband to walk out and leave me. It was wrong for him to just file for divorce. And my human nature (initially) was to just punch his lights out if I ever saw him again. But that would not be reflecting who I am in Christ. And that is my highest goal, so in order to do that I need to respond as He would, and that means **I give up my right to retaliate with a duty to forgive**. That is what forgiveness is . . . it means to give up the right to retaliate.

Forgiveness is not a feeling . . . it is a choice. If we waited until we felt like forgiving, we'd probably never do it. I'm pretty sure Jesus didn't feel like forgiving us, but He did it because He knew it would please His Father in heaven, which was His ultimate goal. And forgiveness takes time. If you have been deeply hurt, don't beat yourself up because you have not yet forgiven. Again, it takes time to get to that point. I learned through the DivorceCare[2] class that sometimes the first step is to pray and ask God to make us willing to be willing to think about forgiving.

There is so much freedom when we forgive. It feels like the weight of the world has been lifted off of me because I have given my ex-husband over to God. I now can actually pray for him, that God will bless him and his life. I found it is hard to hate someone I am praying for. So now that I have forgiven him, I am free to move on with my life, and God has, and I believe will continue, to bless my obedience.

Forgiveness does not mean there won't be consequences for the wrongs done against us. It means we give up any control of that and trust God will take care of that. In Romans 12:19, it says, "*Do not take revenge, my friends, but leave room for God's wrath, for it is written, It is mine to avenge; I will repay says the Lord*", so trust Him to issue a punishment if He deems necessary.

Forgiveness does not mean you have to forget the offense. Only God can truly forget wrongs done against Him. We are human so things are going to happen to trigger a memory. But I believe when that happens, we have to choose to forgive **again**. In Matthew 18:22, it says that we are to "*forgive 7 x 70 times*" and I believe that is in the Bible for such times as these.

During the Divorce Recovery class I was attending, I heard someone say that un-forgiveness can block the blessings God wants to give to us! Yikes! I certainly don't want that. I want all the blessings God wants to give me, so this was an incentive for me.

But the biggest incentive for me to forgive is found in Matthew 6:14-15, where Jesus said, "*For if you forgive men when they sin against you, your Heavenly Father will also forgive you. BUT if you do not forgive men their sins, your Father will not forgive your sins*". This to me is one of the scariest passages in the Bible. I definitely want God to forgive me, so the only guarantee I have of that is for me to forgive others.

So let me now tell you about that early Christmas present I mentioned earlier. It was about three weeks before Christmas when I was at work and my cell phone rang. I normally don't answer it at work but this caller called twice so I immediately thought it could be one of my daughters, possibly in trouble using a friend's phone. So I answered it. The voice on the other end identified himself as my ex-husband. I didn't even recognize his voice! Now I hadn't seen him or talked to him in almost four years, so this was quite unexpected, and I was, believe it or not, speechless.

He said, "Can you talk?" And I eventually mustered up the strength to breath and speak and say, "No, I'm at work," so he said, "OK, I'll call back and leave a message." About 20 minutes later or so, I checked the message, and it was my ex-husband telling me about his parent's 50th wedding anniversary party and how nice it was. Then he just broke down crying. I mean this man was sobbing! It was heartbreaking. Through his sobs I could barely make out he was saying what a mistake he had made leaving me and he was stupid (and I think he said that more than once, but whose counting). He hoped someday I could think about forgiving him. Then he cried harder to where he was just blubbering and I could barely understand him. I heard him say he had made a huge mistake. He remembered how on the day he left I had begged him to stay, and how he regretted his decision to leave. Then he just said, "I'm sorry I bothered you . . ." and hung up.

Now in 8 ½ years of marriage, I only recall seeing him cry twice, so this was very out of character for him. But here is the cool thing – I got absolutely no pleasure hearing him this desperate. It truly hurt my heart to hear someone in so much pain, and I didn't have to think for a second what I should do. I knew I needed to let him know I'd already forgiven him. God was giving me the chance to imitate Christ to my ex-husband! So I emailed him right away and told him I had forgiven him and told him I'd be praying for him.

See, the gift was that I, for a moment, got to reflect my God! Instead of getting even with my ex-husband for many past hurts, I was given the opportunity to reflect God's grace through forgiveness. And it felt wonderful! I could almost sense God was looking down on me with a smile on His face saying, "Yep, that's my girl and I am so pleased."

Our human nature does not really understand forgiveness. Instead we want revenge and justice. Forgiveness goes against our fleshly nature, so when we are able to do it, there really isn't any other explanation other than God's power is at work in us. I love that thought . . . the same power that raised Jesus from the dead is working inside of us! Amen!

So how do you know if you have truly forgiven someone? Well I believe some indications are when you have a peace in your heart, your worship is real and meaningful, when you have joy in your life. If someone has hurt you and you are holding on to bitterness or anger, it is not hurting them. It is ultimately hurting you. I heard someone say that not forgiving is like drinking poison and expecting another person to get sick from it. By not forgiving, you are giving that person power over you, and you will be miserable.

When I finished my talk that day in Poland, I was so relieved knowing my sessions were over so there was no more pressure. Now I could just sit back, relax, and enjoy the remainder of the conference. Until the next morning that is, when I was asked to speak on Forgiveness again. Yikes! So that afternoon, I spoke on forgiveness again, and at the end, one of the ladies told me (through an interpreter) that her niece was going through a divorce so could she have a copy of my notes to share with her. I gave her all of them. It was an honor to be able to share with her.

XX

All About Me

In order to fully heal, move on with my life, and possibly be in a relationship again some day, it is important for me to take a good look at me and my role in my failed marriage(s). I would suggest you do the same. This is not easy, because I want to instead think I did nothing wrong. I want to believe I was the victim here and lay ALL the blame on my spouse(s) who left. But we know none of us are perfect. I'm not saying anything I (or you) did wrong deserved our spouse's decision to just up and leave. But to keep from making the same mistakes over again, I need to look at my part, learn from it, and make any necessary changes. (As I think about this, I realize I made the same mistakes with both marriages. I'm a slow learner.)

In my case, I believe my whole goal in life was for my husband to be happy. This may sound like a noble goal for a wife, but the problem is that no person can make another person totally happy. That is just too much responsibility for any one person. Happiness often comes from our circumstances while joy comes from a right relationship with God. I thought that as long as I was doing my share (or more at times) it would make him happy. That in turn would make him happy with me and he wouldn't be able to live without me. In essence, I thought I needed to *earn* his love. Talk about having some self-esteem issues! (We could talk about that in a whole other chapter, and it may take a whole chapter!)

Instead, a spouse should be a best friend, supporter and encourager. If that means calling them out on an issue, do that comfortably in love. We need to hold each other accountable so we are living the best life we can. Even though it is often uncomfortable and even painful to do this, it is often the most loving thing we can do to encourage the other person to get back on the right track. (If you are dreading doing such a thing, your motives are probably pure.) If I see someone about to step into oncoming traffic, the most loving thing I can do is to pull them back on the sidewalk or get their attention so they don't get hit by a car. In the same way, if I ignore the sin of my spouse because I am afraid he'll be mad at me temporarily, I am allowing him to get hit by Satan and his schemes.

I didn't realize the importance of accountability and was afraid in both marriages that if I confronted my husbands, they would get angry with me, withhold love from me and possibly leave – my biggest fear. Isn't that interesting? And look where I am now by not taking this responsibility in marriage, I am exactly where I didn't want to be. I've also learned that fear has no place in a marriage relationship.

Instead I wanted to keep the peace at all cost. Sometimes the most loving thing I could have done was to speak up.

Instead, I skirted around the issues and "walked on eggshells" pretending all was OK. I often times allowed his mood to determine mine. I have recently learned I cannot control anyone else (not a spouse, or a child, a co-worker, or friend). I only have control over me. I need to learn how to confront in love, and then not allow that person's attitude to change mine.

The other problem was I unconsciously put my husband before God. I made him my god or idol, and as long as he was pleased with me, I was happy and content. But that could change at any moment. God is not like that at all. God is the perfect love, and no matter what I've done, nothing can separate me from the love of God. Did you get that? *Nothing* can separate me (or you) from the love of God, according to Romans 8:39. And I don't have to earn His love . . . it is a gift. How freeing is that? Now this doesn't mean I can live any way I want to, but instead it means when I fail (and we all do) He still loves us. There will still be consequences when we make unwise decisions, but we are still loved. I heard Liz Curtis Higgs explain in her Bible study entitled, *Loved by God*, [33] that God doesn't love us any more when we are good, because He already loves us completely! Amazing!

I believe toward the end of my marriage, my husband didn't feel I respected him. This makes me sad. In the Bible when it talks about marriage, husbands are commanded to **love** their wives and wives are commanded to **respect** their husbands because God knows what each of us needs to the core of our being and what each sex struggles with.

I loved my husband and respected him, but maybe in hindsight he needed to hear that. Maybe my actions didn't indicate this often enough. Maybe I would have been respecting him more by taking up for myself or my kids instead of backing down (most of the time) and giving in to keep the peace. Lord, forgive me.

My other mistake, I believe, is being very independent. Again, this sounds like a positive, and it can be. However, I thought asking my husband to help me with anything would be a bother or inconvenience to him, so I unconsciously communicated I didn't need him. I thought that was OK. In fact, I thought it was better because it meant I wanted him. But I guess everyone wants to be needed as well.

Questions to ponder:

1) What was your part in the failed marriage?
2) What can you learn from this and how can you change?
3) Pray and ask God to forgive you for your part, and then believe He has and forgive yourself.

June 4, 2009

Keeping the financial books for PROeM (the ministry in Poland) allowed me to meet a local music producer. I sheepishly told him about the song God had given me and asked for advice on how to get some music recorded for it. He told me he already had a studio booked in a couple of weeks in Nashville, and to email him my acapella version. He said he'd write some music and have the musicians play it at the end of their already scheduled recording session. He would send that recording to me so I could practice with it, and then I could record the vocals at his local studio.

How exciting!!! So I emailed it to him and I anxiously await his "mix".

June 19, 2009

Today I received the recorded "mix" of the music to my song, and it is great! It is a little jazzier than I had envisioned, but I like it so much! The musicians who played on it include a guitar player for Gretchen Wilson. Another one of the musicians plays in the Christian band Sonic Flood. How cool is that?! Now I get to practice singing with it and in a few weeks, I'll go to the studio and record the vocals. Am I dreaming?

Sunday, June 21, 2009

I am lonely today and feel a little unloved. It is Father's Day. My dad died 13 years ago, my step-dad is out of town, and my father-in-law will probably be visited by my ex-husband, so there is no one for me to celebrate the occasion with. I sit here by myself. Alone. But maybe in these times of being by myself, God is even closer than I know. I believe the Bible with my whole heart, so I know He is with me because it says He will never leave me nor forsake me. I am thankful, but sometimes I want someone with some skin on.

I've been thinking a lot lately about this big dream of my book. I am reading a book entitled, *The Dream Giver*, [49] and in church today, a video clip was shown. The young man in the video said, "Don't give up on your dream." Really? Was that just for me, God? Last night I read about how we each have a dream in our heart and if we don't accomplish it, we are just merely living. I don't want that. I want my life (failures and all) to count! I want to leave a legacy! I want to be a blessing! But I'm a little afraid because the chapter I'm on in the book asked what I have to give up to live my dream, and frankly I don't know. It seems like initially I need to spend a lot of time writing and researching. OK I can live with that; I just need to give up some TV time or a few outings. Then the next step involves editing and finding a publisher. I'm praying for the Holy Spirit to be my agent and to put the correct people in my path at the right time, because I have absolutely no idea how to do this.

But then I realized my dream is more than just writing the book; my dream is that God would use my story to persuade people that through Him there is healing and hope for their lives! What if that entails me having to market the book and do signings and travel and speak about it? Yikes! How exciting, but at the same time, how scary! And then there could be that constant temptation of pride and for me to think I am "all that and a bag of chips" when that is really not my goal at all. My goal is to glorify God, and I am most able to do that when I am weak. Then His strength becomes evident.

What if this schedule keeps me from dating and getting married again some day? I so desire this! I long to love and be loved and to invest in someone else. What if he has children? How cool to be a part of their lives? But what if this is part of the cost of my dream? What if I am to remain single for the rest of my life? Can I do it, and consider it a gift and glorify God through it?

I went on a walk tonight and toward the end saw a rainbow! It had not rained since about 10:00 a.m. and it was 9:00 p.m. when I saw the rainbow! I took it as a sign from

God of His promise to be with me and guide me, and that when I seek Him with all my heart, I'll find Him. Yes! That is what I want more than anything.

Lord I truly want only Your will for my life, even if it includes being single forever (that was really hard to type) because I know Your plan for me is better than any I can come up with. If that is Your will, please truly allow my head and my heart to accept it. And is it OK to ask You to help my heart to not hurt?

The Dating Game

August 1, 2010

Wow, it has been over a year since I have journaled. I really wish I could tell you that having worked so hard on healing and becoming the best woman I can be, I have met a wonderful man who God has prepared for me, and we're getting married and will live happily ever after. But, the reality is that after being single for almost six years, I am still single and content. Well, I'm content most of the time, but recently, the subject of dating has emerged. Yikes!

A very nice guy recently asked me out via email and I immediately thought "no" so I responded to his email (which took me an hour to compose) letting him know that it wasn't about him; I just wasn't quite ready. The next day I told my friend, LuAnn, about it as we walked the neighborhood and she said, in the most loving way, "It does not take most people five years to heal. You have done a great job and worked hard, but maybe it is OK to go out."

This got me to thinking, "Why am I not ready?" I think there are two reasons. One is because I don't understand dating. After talking with my counselor about this, she informed me there are several kinds of dating. Going out with someone can just be a fun thing to do to get to know someone. It doesn't mean I have to marry him. This is a new concept to me because I've only dated three guys and married two of them! I'm not sure I can do this because I have a tendency to get attached, which leads to my other reason for avoiding dating: fear of being rejected. My life experience with this has been that, eventually, they choose someone else over me. I'm just not sure my heart can handle that again. How many times is a heart supposed to be broken? God has healed my heart and I am beyond thankful, but I just don't want to go through it again.

There are several books on this subject and some say it is OK to just date for fun and meet people and learn about yourself. Others talk about living your life as God would have you to, and if He has a mate for you, He'll allow your paths to cross. Both concepts are from Christian authors, so I am confused on which is best for me. I know I can't just sit around and hope God will bring me a date via UPS, but I wonder if it is enough to be involved in the different ministries God has allowed me to be involved in, while living my life and doing fun things like going to concerts and singles events. Am I supposed to go online or attend a singles class to find a date? Sigh. Obviously I do not know enough to write on this subject, so instead, I'll just list some books that come highly recommended.

How To Get A Date Worth Keeping, by Dr. Henry Cloud
Boundaries in Dating, by Dr. Henry Cloud and Dr. John Townsend
God is A Matchmaker, by Derek Prince
Date or Soul Mate, by Neil Clark Warren, PhD

After a discussion with my counselor on dating, she suggested I read *Right People Right Place Right Plan*, by Jentezen Franklin. (What a cool name.) In a chapter where he talks about how God redeems and restores us, he also says, "I assure you God has destined someone to love you. Rest assured he or she is living and breathing right now somewhere on this planet. He or she is going to love God and love you passionately. Your job is to trust God and from this day forward keep yourself just for that special someone God will send to you." Then later in the chapter he says, "God said that it is not good for man to be alone, so most likely, it is His will for you to marry. You may ask, what about Paul? He was single, yes, but unless you've given yourself so fully to God's work that you have no desire to be married, then God has someone for you when the time is right." [50] I like this thought.

My problem, as diagnosed by my brilliant counselor, is I really don't know how to interact with single, available men. I'm blaming the fact I attended an all-girl high school, thank you very much! (I did get a great education, though.) She suggested I take an inventory and write down all the good and bad things about the past men in my life. Then grieve them, forgive them, and move on. Dang, sounds like a lot of work. She explained I am probably avoiding men by staying busy. Really? Here I am thinking I'm doing good stuff by facilitating the Divorce Recovery classes at two churches, teaching high school girls Sunday school classes, teaching a ladies Bible study in the Spring at my church, and singing on our worship team once a month. They are all good, and I thoroughly enjoy each of them, but wonder if I have really sought God's guidance in doing all this. Am I subconsciously doing all of this to avoid the singles scene? Are you? What are we going to do about that?

Mistakes Women Often Make

August 8, 2010

Last week I was listening to the *New Life* [53] call-in radio show, and a female caller told the radio counselors she had been married and divorced four times. Trying to get to the bottom of why she had made so many poor choices, one of the counselors asked her about her childhood. She explained her father had been an alcoholic and had beaten her mom, so she had decided at an early age to not marry a man with these two defects. The radio host then said the coolest thing, which I'd never thought of. He said instead of setting her standards high, like God has for her, (and for each of us) she settled for men who *just* did not drink and did not hit her. These men lacked character in other areas. I had never thought of that before and wanted to include it to give you (and me) something to think about.

Also, I've learned a man (or a woman) saying they are Christian is not enough. Why do we fall for that so often? I believe having a mate of the same faith is so important, but as we date, we need to look for the fruits of their faith to be sure they aren't just giving lip service about their Christianity. We should look for the "fruit of the spirit" as listed in Galatians 6:22-23. If he is serious about his relationship with God, these will naturally be a part of his daily life; and they should be a part of our daily life as well. This is why it is so important not to rush into a relationship. Anyone can fake "being fruitful" for a while.

August 11, 2010

I arrived at church tonight to facilitate the DivorceCare class. As I was walking through the parking lot, my minister, Rick, saw me and yelled out from his car window. He told me he was going to have a medical test on Thursday, and asked me to pray for him. I told him that, of course, I'd pray for him and then asked him to pray for me because I was going to record my song on the same day. I asked him to keep it on the "down low" because I don't know how it is going to turn out and I don't want to seem prideful. He agreed.

Sunday, Aug 15, 2010

This afternoon right after church, we had a leadership meeting. I was about 20 minutes late because I had promised to give a friend a ride home from church. So I arrived back at church and walked into the meeting and was informed that I hadn't missed too much and we were going to take some prayer requests, and did I have any. I said, "No, I'm good." Rick, our minister, said, "Are you sure?" And I again indicated I had none at this time. He went on to tell the other participants he'd like them to remember him in prayer on Thursday because he was going to have a medical test. Then he turned to me and said, "And you can just **sing** your prayers for me." I know I looked puzzled and everyone in the room had the strangest looks on their faces as they all stared at me. I leaned in to Rick and said, "Did you tell them about the recording?" To which he exclaimed, "Yes, I couldn't help it, I am so excited!" They wanted to know how it all came about and I explained again how God had given me a song. Then, our associate minister said, "This is great! On October 31, our topic is 'The Strong Arm of God' and it is about God's healing, so how about you sing your song that day?" I was stunned, and wondered if I was ready for that, but agreed to do so realizing that maybe it is time to share the song God gave me.

August 19, 2010

This afternoon, I arrived at the recording studio full of nerves and excitement. BJ, the producer, was so kind and reassuring. His studio is set up so I stood on one side of a wall in front of a microphone. I got to wear a headset (oh, how I wish I had a picture of that for my Facebook page – see I'm already struggling with a little pride!) I sang the lyrics several times, making a few changes as he suggested. In less than 30 minutes, I was done. Now I wait for him to combine my vocals with the music mix in Nashville. I can't believe this is happening! Who am I to deserve such favor? This is a dream come true, and I am so thankful for the experience.

October 18, 2010

Today I received the final mix of the song. I was so nervous, but yet excited to hear it for the first time. I let Katie listen to it first and she sat there with tears in her eyes. She is proud of me. That is the best feeling ever! I have always wanted my girls to be proud of me. Thank you, Lord, for that blessing.

October 25, 2010

Today I spoke with my phone counselor and after a few minutes she said, "I have never felt led to say this to you until now, but I believe it is time for you to start praying about dating." Hello, I think you are breaking up, I thought. She explained I seem to have no problem interacting with the men I work with and the men in the DivorceCare classes (maybe because I am the leader, and it is a safe place where we discourage dating so each member can heal). But I seem to be uncomfortable with single men in any other situation. She said I need to learn how to just sit across the table from them in a social situation. Yikes!

She explained because I'm afraid, I am avoidant. I've been thinking about this and I think that for me it has been safer to be in the non-dating state. That way, there is no rejection. If I start letting people know I'm going to start dating, and no one asks me out, that will make me wonder again what is wrong with me. I'm glad her advice was to start *praying* God would open doors in this area instead of having me go to Polka lessons or something ridiculous like that! (Ummm . . . she actually did suggest I take some dancing lessons. Sigh.)

October 31, 2010

Today at church, I gave my testimony about my divorce, the story behind the song, and God's healing in my life. Then I sang my song. I was so nervous! I always hope to do a great job when I sing, but usually I sing songs by other artists (professionals no less) so there is never any fear the congregation will not like them. With my own song, if someone doesn't like it, it would be like having someone tell me my baby was ugly! However, I know it really is not about the song, and that was at the end of my testimony. I told the congregation I hoped when they left today they would take away more than just if they liked or didn't like the song. Most importantly they would remember how God not only removed all my anger, hurt and unforgiveness, but replaced those emotions with joy, peace and excitement for the future. I asked them to consider in the same way what He longs to do for them or through them.

After the service, I received so many nice comments about the song, and it felt great. A couple of people even said it was radio-worthy. One guy suggested I sell it and have someone like Leeann Womack record it. That is so nice, but that really isn't my goal. I really want to be the one to sing it (Lord willing, of course). My brother, the tough one who would beat someone up for me, came that day and cried! He has seen me go through this pain-filled journey, so to see me be able to stand in front of people and be vulnerable and then sing made him proud of me. My favorite comment, though, was from a friend of mine who came up to me with tears in her eyes and said that my obedience to do something with the song encouraged her to be courageous. She plans to start a ministry dear to her heart she has been afraid to do. What an honor she would share that with me!

May, 2012

Wow, it has been a long time since I have journaled; probably because I thought I would have published this by now! Well since I haven't, I'll write about my most recent feelings, which have really caught me off-guard. Nickie has been dating an incredible young man named Justin since January. She met him at college, so they have been friends for almost two years. Since I was able to go and visit her several weekends at school, I have spent time with many of her friends, including him, so I have watched how he interacted with and treated her in the friendship stage. I also got to watch them practice for, and then lead a worship service together, and it touched my heart and brought tears to my eyes. He came to visit us for a few days recently so he could help with and be in attendance at her graduation party. (Side note: one daughter graduated from college, and one to go . . . and she is on track to be done in two years! Yeah! I am so proud!) So after watching them, I feel sort of stupid admitting this, but I want what they have. Don't get me wrong, I am beyond excited for them! They are both wonderful young adults; they have made wise choices and they deserve every blessing God has for them. They have this amazing love and respect for each other, a mutual love for God, they have fun together and can just be themselves around each other. It is the coolest thing to watch. They adore each other. Sigh.

Maybe that is what love is all about, and I feel ridiculous because you'd think since I've been married twice I'd know all about this! But when I think back on my marriages, I respected and loved my husbands, but maybe I was just so desperate to get married, I didn't demand this sort of respect/love in return. Maybe I didn't believe I deserved it. I'm sure they cared for me, but I don't believe they ever cherished or adored me. I don't want to be worshiped, but how cool would it be for someone's face to light up simply because I walked into the room. (Or maybe I'm a certified dreamer . . .or nut!)

So maybe knowing that this actually exists is what it will take to get me out into the dating world. See, I like to think that I am strong – "I am woman hear me roar" and I don't *need* a guy; that it is a sign of weakness to desire one. But maybe instead my pride could be keeping me from a blessing God has for me? Maybe He even designed me this way? Maybe He really has someone out there for me who loves Him with his whole heart, whom I could worship with and serve alongside. Maybe it is time for me to put the energy that I have put into these last "parenting" years into a new relationship for my future. Help me, Jesus! Now don't get me wrong, I have no regrets about not dating and instead healing and pouring my energy into my daughters' lives these last few years, as I wouldn't trade the relationship I have with them for anything in this world. But maybe like Rafiki said in Disney's movie, *The Lion King*, [57] "It is time." But, I am scared! What if I get hurt again? Or what if no one wants to go out with me? Is it better to take the chance and be disappointed, or worse, hurt, or is it better to be safe and stay to myself? This is the battle that wars within me.

So God, I ask you for your guidance and wisdom and even protection. Help me to make wise choices and not to just settle. Help me to remember I am worth being pursued. Help me to enjoy the whole dating process, to just have fun and meet people and experience new things like snowboarding, for example, and to not just focus on meeting "the one", in case there isn't one. And if there isn't, please help me to be content in this singleness. Amen.

Consequences

Although God has healed my heart, please don't think I *never* struggle with anything related to my divorces, because although the incidences are few and far between now, I do. In fact, as I helped Nickie pack up her dorm room before graduating, a part of me was a little mad that her dad wasn't there to celebrate her academic accomplishments . . . and help me carry all her possessions down three flights of stairs. Not that I minded helping, but this should be a family event, so as I watched other fathers helping their children, a place in my heart hurt knowing my daughters will never have that. (Plus that couch was heavy!) It is a consequence of divorce that I, and, unfortunately, my daughters as well, will have to deal with.

Another consequence of divorce continues to be loneliness. Now although my life is good, I do have some lonely times. Recently I felt especially lonely when I saw an adorable couple at church holding hands and making goo-goo eyes at one another. On my way home, I decided to get some comfort food to help fill that lonely place in my heart, so I ordered a Big Mac (but no fries so it would be a healthier meal that way. Right.) When I got home, I noticed that the drive-thru employee had mistakenly put fries in my bag, too, so I ate every last one convinced God wanted me to have them to comfort my lonely soul. Is He amazing or what?!

And I have longed for a mate to help advise me during these last few years of parenting. It is so hard to do alone; I just wasn't wired to be both a mom and a dad. But I do the best I can and pray for God's wisdom, and ask for His grace when I fail.

Loneliness has especially hit since several weeks ago, Nickie moved to another state because she got a job there. I am so excited for her and for her future, but she has become more than just my daughter; she has become a best friend.

I miss her like crazy. Walking past her empty room is so hard! I know I am grieving because, although I am happy for her, it is a loss for me not having her to do life with. Coming home at the end of my workday to an empty home is tough, as Katie is not home much since she is attending classes at the University of Kentucky. On the nights I do not have plans, I have such good intentions of exercising or doing simple little home repairs. But some times I just can't muster up the energy. This is just part of the grieving process, which I know is normal, but that doesn't make it any easier. I know when those days are upon me, I just need to deal with the sadness, cry like a baby, call a friend, and go on. (Or maybe I'll get a dog. Not.)

I believe this "letting go of our kids process" is more difficult for a single parent. At least as a married couple, there is someone there to grieve with, talk to, comfort you, or just hold you while you cry, or take you out to eat! But as a single parent, we experience the grieving at the same time as the loneliness, and it is especially tough.

I know this, too, will pass, and maybe this loneliness will force me out of my comfort zone some. Maybe I'll start a new hobby, take a class, or check out a singles group and meet new people. (Maybe I'll write a sequel on this topic!) I have to remember that life is not supposed to be happy every day. Whether married or not, emotions like sadness and loneliness are normal and a part of life. Maybe they even help us to appreciate the good times more.

XXI

My Final Thoughts

By reading this book, you know me, and you know I am just an ordinary (and most of the time ridiculous) woman. But God is using me in ways I'd never even dreamed of. He has taken this shy woman to Poland to *speak* at two women's conferences. He has put a passion in my heart for the people hurting from separation and divorce, and has not only given me that ministry at my church, but at another local church as well. He has totally healed my heart. Truly I have not one ounce of hate, jealously, bitterness or anger toward my ex-husband, so I can pray for a blessed life for him. And God has filled my life with the most incredible friends, many whom I would not have known had divorce not been a part of my story.

I say all of this to encourage you in your healing. Remember that your divorce does not have to define you. It is an incident in your life, so my prayer is you'll take the time to work through the healing process. I don't believe time alone heals all wounds. Remember, I was single for five years before I started dating my second husband, but during that time I was too busy working two jobs and raising my young daughters to even know I needed to work on healing. This is why I highly recommend you attend the DivorceCare workshop in your area. And remember, this time alone is not a waste. As one of the participants in the DivorceCare[2] DVD said, "It is actually a gift". It is time I have spent in God's word, saturating myself with His truths. I am also learning who I am and discovering the dreams in my heart. For the first time in my life, I am confident in who I am . . . most days.

You probably noticed that my journaling time became less frequent as the time went by and I healed, as I've been busy living my life and pondering my future instead of focusing on the past. That is a good sign. But since I'm no longer in a desperate place of pain, I have to admit I don't spend as much time with God as I did. (Maybe that is why I haven't been given another song yet.) So this is an area I need to work on, because I don't want to ever lose that closeness. I don't ever want to get to a place where I think I am self-sufficient and don't need Him. God forbid it! I want God's will in my life, and recently heard in a message from Kyle Idleman (the Teaching Minister at SECC) that God is more concerned with who I am growing to become than in where I live or what I do.

My life is rich and most of the time, fun! I am enjoying an amazing journey with my daughters, family and friends, and I am beyond grateful to God for His blessings and grace. Thank you so much for following my journey. My prayer is that somehow God can use my story to give you hope. Even though you will experience some tough days, He longs to heal you, and as it says in Job 42:12, "*Bless the later years more than your first.*" You, too, can have a song to sing!

The End . . . or is it just the beginning . . .

References

[1] Casting Crowns, "Slow Fade", *The Alter and The Door*, 2007.

[2] Church Initiative, Inc. *Divorce Care.* Wake Forest: 2004. DVD.

[3] Building 429, "Glory Defined," *Space In Between Us*, 2005.

[4] Chris Tomlin, "Holy Is The Lord," *Arriving*, 2004.

[5] Beth Moore, *When Godly People do Ungodly Things* (Nashville: Broadman & Holman, 2002).

[6] Chris Tomlin, *The Way I Was Made* (Sisters, Ore.: Multnomah Publishers, Inc., 2005), 130.

[7] Chris Tomlin, "Captured," *The Noise We Make*, 2001.

[8] Chris Tomlin, *The Way I Was Made* (Sisters, Ore.: Multnomah Publishers, Inc., 2005), 133.

[9] Chris Tomlin, "Overflow," *Not To Us,* 2002.

[10] Chris Tomlin, *The Way I Was Made* (Sisters, Ore.: Multnomah Publishers, Inc., 2005).

[11] Dee Brestin & Kathy Troccoli, *Falling In Love With Jesus* (Nashville: W Publishing Group, 2001).

[12] Passion Worship Band, "My Glorious," *Our Love Is Loud*, 2002.

[13] Dee Brestin & Kathy Troccoli, *Forever In Love With Jesus* (Nashville: W Publishing Group, 2004)

[14] Chris Tomlin, *The Way I Was Made* (Sisters, Ore.: Multnomah Publishers, Inc., 2005)

[15] Louie Gigleo, *The Air I Breathe* (Sisters, Ore.: Multnomah Publishers, Inc., 2003)

[16] Chris Tomlin, *The Way I Was Made* (Sisters, Ore.: Multnomah Publishers, Inc., 2005), 143.

[17] Chris Tomlin, *The Way I Was Made* (Sisters, Ore.: Multnomah Publishers, Inc., 2005), 143.

[18] Louie Gigleo, *The Air I Breathe* (Sisters, Ore.: Multnomah Publishers, Inc., 2003)

[19] Henry Cloud & John Townsend, *God Will Make A Way* (Brentwood, TN: Integrity Publishers, 2003)

[20] Henry Cloud & John Townsend, *God Will Make A Way* (Brentwood, TN: Integrity Publishers, 2003)

[21] Beth Moore, *The Patriarchs Bible Study* (Nashville: LifeWay Press, 2005)

[22] Beth Moore, *The Patriarchs Bible Study* DVD (Nashville: LifeWay Press, 2005)

[23] Henry Cloud & John Townsend, *God Will Make A Way* (Brentwood, TN: Integrity Publishers, 2003)

[24] The Passion of the Christ, DVD, Twentieth Century Fox, Directed by Mel Gibson, 2004.

[25] Beth Moore, *The Patriarchs Bible Study* DVD (Nashville: LifeWay Press, 2005)

[26] Beth Moore, *The Patriarchs Bible Study* DVD (Nashville: LifeWay Press, 2005)

[27] Beth Moore, *The Patriarchs Bible Study* DVD (Nashville: LifeWay Press, 2005)

[28] Chris Tomlin, "Everything", *Not To Us*, 2002.

[29] Beth Moore, *The Patriarchs Bible Study* DVD (Nashville: LifeWay Press, 2005)

[30] Avalon, "Orphans of God," *Stand*, 2006.

[31] Sheila Walsh, *Life is Tough But God is Faithful* (Nashville: Thomas Nelson Publishing, 1999)

[32] Louie Gigleo, *Indescribable* DVD, 2009.

[33] Liz Curtis Higgs, *Loved by God Bible Study* DVD (Dallas: Sampson Resources, 2004)

[34] Delirious, "Rain Down", *Grace Like A River*, 2004.

[35] Tommy Walker, "He Knows My Name".

[36] Cockrel, Lisa Ann. "Mountain Mover." Today's Christian Woman. September 2006: Print.

[37] Chris Tomlin, "Amazing Grace My Chains Are Gone", *See The Morning*, 2006.

[38] Switchfoot, "Dare You To Move," *The Beautiful Letdown*, 2004.

[39] Eastman Curtis, *Pursuing Your Life Dream* (Tulsa, OK.: Harrison House, Inc., 2002) PG 113.

[40] Eastman Curtis, *Pursuing Your Life Dream* (Tulsa, OK.: Harrison House, Inc., 2002) PG 104.

[41] Eastman Curtis, *Pursuing Your Life Dream* (Tulsa, OK.: Harrison House, Inc., 2002) PG 104.

[42] Church Initiative, Inc. *Divorce Care.* Wake Forest: 2004. Print.

[43] Jeremy Camp, "Give You Glory," *Beyond Measure*, 2006

[44] Bruce Wilkinson, *The Prayer of Jabez (*Sisters, Ore.: Multnomah Publishers, Inc., 2000)

[45] John Eldridge, *Journey of Desire* (Nashville: Thomas Nelson Publishing, 2000)

[46] John & Stasi Eldredge, *Captivating* (Nashville: Thomas Nelson Publishing, 2005)

[47] Mark Schultz, "You Are A Child Of Mine," *Stories & Songs*, 2003.

[48] Jeremy Camp, "Walk by Faith," *Stay*, 2004.

[49] Bruce Wilkinson, *The Dream Giver* (Sisters, Ore.: Multnomah Publishers, Inc., 2003

[50] Jentezen Franklin, *Right People Right Place Right Plan* (New Kensington, PA: Whitaker House, 2007)

[51] Hillsong, *United We Stand*, 2006.

[52] *Living On The Edge*. Salem. WFIA, Louisville. 12 April 2005. Radio.

[53] *New Life*, Salem. WFIA, Louisville. Radio.

[54] *Focus On The Family*, Salem. WFIA, Louisville. 25 July 2006. Radio

[55] *Heart of Worship*, Salem. WAY-FM, Louisville. 13 August 2006. Radio

[56] Bruce Wilkinson, *The Prayer of Jabez* (Sisters: Multnomah Publishers, 2000)

[57] *The Lion King*. Directed by Roger Allers and Rob Minkoff. 1994. Orlando, Florida: Walt Disney Studios, 2011. DVD.

"I Stand Amazed" music mixed by B J Davis Music, Louisville, KY

Book edited by Amy Board Higgs, Wright Is Might Louisville, LLC, and by Lenisa Alvey, Louisville, KY

Cover designed by Gretchen Allie, Johnson City, TN, Gretchen.Allie@yahoo.com

Photo by Whitney Knutson Photography

Visit my blog at Annette8788.wordpress.com

Acknowledgements

There are so many people whom I would like to thank for their love, friendship and encouragement. They include my family; my daughters, Katie and Nickie; my mom and her husband, Jim; my brothers, Frank and his wife, Donna; Jimmy, and his wife, Beth. Facilitators who helped me through the healing process, and encouraged me to facilitate/ facilitate with me: Alex, Jeff, Linda, Lynda, Yvonne, David, Jan, Jamie, Carrie. Friends who held me when I cried, laughed with me, and encouraged me to complete this project including: LuAnn, Lenisa, Janice, Gina, Mary, Cindy, Karen, Christy, Sandy, Barbara & Stan, Steve, PJ, Angela, Chase, my phone counselor Debbie, Wendy, Bette, Iris and my small group.

I thank my bosses and co-workers for allowing me to have the best job ever, and for modeling generosity so beautifully.

I thank my minister, Rick Burdette, and my Fern Creek Christian Church family. So many of you have poured into me and encouraged me, and I am forever grateful to be part of a family who desires to follow Jesus and disciple others in that walk. Thank you for never treating me like a second-class citizen due to being divorced, but for instead lifting me up and allowing and supporting divorce recovery efforts.

And most importantly, I thank God for seeking me, and for His grace, forgiveness, kindness and outrageous blessings. May this story of my journey really point to His provision and healing power! To God be the glory!

Proceeds from the sale of this book will go to organizations including PROeM's Ministry in Poland, Cure International, Fern Creek Christian Church, Rapha House, Team Expansion, Food for the Poor, and others whose mission is not only to tell about Jesus, but are being His "hands and feet".

CPSIA information can be obtained at www.ICGtesting.com
Printed in the USA
LVOW06s0717310813

350251LV00001B/18/P